THE RED LETTER PLAYS

THE RED LETTER PLAYS

SUZAN-LORI PARKS

Theatre Communications Group
New York

The Red Letter Plays is published by Theatre Communications Group, Inc., 520 8th Ave., New York, NY 10018–4156.

This publication is made possible in part with public funds from the New York State Council on the Arts, a State Agency.

TCG books are exclusively distributed to the book trade by Consortium Book Sales and Distribution, 1045 Westgate Dr., St. Paul, MN 55114.

Library of Congress Cataloging-in-Publication Data
Parks, Suzan-Lori.
The red letter plays / Suzan-Lori Parks.— 1st ed.
p. cm.
Contents: In the blood — Fucking A.
ISBN-10: 1-55936-195-6 (alk. paper)
ISBN-13: 978-1-55936-195-8
1. Afro-American women—Drama. 2. Hawthorne, Nathaniel, 1804–1864—
Adaptations.
I. Hawthorne, Nathaniel, 1804–1864. Scarlet letter. II Title.
PS3566.A736 R44   2000
812'.54—dc21   00-046679

Cover photo of Charlayne Woodard by Martha Swope
Cover design by Pentagram
Text design and composition by Lisa Govan

First Edition, July 2001
Third Printing, May 2007

Thanks 2

Terry Nemeth @ TCG Books

George C. Wolfe and The Posse @ The Public

Kathy Sova
Liz Diamond
David Esbjornson
Loris Bradley, Jason Nodler & IBP
Emily Morse
Dare Clubb
Tony Kushner
John Dias
Bonnie Metzgar
Stephanie Parks
Paul Oscher

4

handholding
cheerleading
loving
& lighthousing

Contents

Author's Elements of Style

I'm continuing the use of my slightly unconventional theatrical elements. Here's a road map.

- *(Rest)*
  Take a little time, a pause, a breather; make a transition.

- A Spell
  An elongated and heightened *(Rest)*. Denoted by repetition of figures' names with no dialogue. Has sort of an architectural look:

Reverend D.
Hester
Reverend D.
Hester

This is a place where the figures experience their pure true simple state. While no action or stage business is necessary, directors should fill this moment as they best see fit.

- [Brackets in the text indicate optional cuts for production.]

- (Parentheses around dialogue indicate softly spoken passages ((asides; sotto voce))).

IN THE BLOOD

Production History

In the Blood premiered at The Joseph Papp Public Theater/
New York Shakespeare Festival (George C. Wolfe, Producer;
Rosemarie Tichler, Artistic Producer; Mark Litvin, Managing
Director) in New York City in November 1999. It was directed
by David Esbjornson; the set design was by Narelle Sissons;
the lighting design was by Jane Cox; the sound design was by
Don DiNicola; the costume design was by Elizabeth Hope
Clancy; the production dramaturg was John Dias; and the pro-
duction stage manager was Kristen Harris. The cast was as
follows:

Hester, La Negrita	Charlayne Woodard
Chilli/Jabber	Rob Campbell
Reverend D./Baby	Reggie Montgomery
The Welfare Lady/Bully	Gail Grate
The Doctor/Trouble	Bruce MacVittie
Amiga Gringa/Beauty	Deirdre O'Connell

Characters

Hester, La Negrita
Chilli/Jabber, her oldest son
Reverend D./Baby, her youngest son
The Welfare Lady/Bully, her oldest daughter
The Doctor/Trouble, her middle son
Amiga Gringa/Beauty, her youngest daughter

Place

Here

Time

Now

Author's Note

This play requires a cast of six adult actors, five of whom double as adults and children. The setting should be spare, to reflect the poverty of the world of the play.

Prologue

All
THERE SHE IS!
WHO DOES SHE THINK
SHE IS
THE NERVE SOME PEOPLE HAVE
SHOULDNT HAVE IT IF YOU CANT AFFORD IT
AND YOU KNOW SHE CANT
SHE DONT GOT NO SKILLS
CEPT ONE
CANT READ CANT WRITE
SHE MARRIED?
WHAT DO YOU THINK?
SHE OUGHTA BE MARRIED
THATS WHY THINGS ARE BAD LIKE THEY ARE
CAUSE OF
GIRLS LIKE THAT
THAT EVER HAPPEN TO ME YOU WOULDNT SEE ME
    HAVING IT
YOU WOULDNT SEE THAT HAPPENING TO ME
WHO THE HELL SHE THINK SHE IS
AND NOW WE GOT TO PAY FOR IT
THE NERVE
SOME PEOPLE HAVE
BAD LUCK
SHE OUGHTA GET MARRIED
TO WHO?
THIS AINT THE FIRST TIME THIS HAS HAPPENED
    TO HER

NO?
THIS IS HER FIFTH
FIFTH?
SHE GOT FIVE OF THEM
FIVE BRATS
AND NOT ONE OF THEM GOT A DADDY
PAH!

They spit.

WHOS THE DADDY?
SHE WONT TELL
SHE WONT TELL CAUSE SHE DONT KNOW
SHE KNOWS
NO SHE DONT
HOW COULD A GIRL NOT KNOW
WHEN YOU HAD SO MUCH ACTION YOU LOSE A
    FRACTION
OF YR GOOD SENSE
THE PART OF MEN SHE SEES ALL LOOK THE SAME
    ANYWAY
WATCH YR MOUTH
I DIDNT SAY NOTHING
YOU TALKING ALL NASTY AND THAT AINT RIGHT
THERES CHILDREN HERE
WHERES THE CHILDREN I DONT SEE NO CHILDREN
SHE MARRIED?
SHE AINT MARRIED
SHE DONT GOT NO SKILLS
CEPT ONE
CANT READ CANT WRITE
SHE MARRIED?
WHAT DO YOU THINK?

All
All
All

SHE KNOWS SHES A NO COUNT
SHIFTLESS
HOPELESS
BAD NEWS

BURDEN TO SOCIETY
HUSSY
SLUT
PAH!

> They spit.

JUST PLAIN STUPID IF YOU ASK ME AINT NO SMART
    WOMAN GOT 5 BASTARDS
AND NOT A PENNY TO HER NAME
SOMETHINGS GOTTA BE DONE TO STOP THIS SORT
    OF THING
CAUSE I'LL BE DAMNED IF SHE GONNA LIVE OFF ME
HERE SHE COMES
MOVE ASIDE
WHAT SHE GOTS CATCHY
LET HER PASS
DONT GET CLOSE
YOU DONT WANNA LOOK LIKE YOU KNOW HER
STEP OFF!

> They part like the Red Sea would.
> Hester, La Negrita passes through them.
> She holds a Newborn Baby in her arms.

All
IT WONT END WELL FOR HER
HOW YOU KNOW?
I GOT EYES DON'T I
BAD NEWS IN HER BLOOD
PLAIN AS DAY.

All
Hester
All

> Hester lifts the child up, raising it toward the sky.

Hester
My treasure. My joy.

All
PAH!

> They spit.

SCENE 1
Under the Bridge

> Home under the bridge. The word "SLUT" scrawled on a wall. Hesters oldest child Jabber, 13, studies that scrawl. Hester lines up soda cans as her youngest child Baby, 2 years old, watches.

Hester
Zit uh good word or a bad word?

Jabber
Jabber

Hester
Aint like you to have yr mouth shut, Jabber. Say it to me and we can figure out the meaning together.

Jabber
Naaaa —

Hester
What I tell you bout saying "Naa" when you mean "no"? You talk like that people wont think you got no brains and Jabbers got brains. All my kids got brains, now.
(Rest)
Lookie here, Baby. Mamma set the cans for you. Mamma gonna show you how to make some money. Watch.

Jabber
Im slow.

Hester

Slow aint never stopped nothing, Jabber. You bring yr foot down on it and smash it flat. Howabout that, Baby? Put it in the pile and thats that. Now you try.

> Baby jumps on the can smashing it flat,
> hollering as he smashes.

Baby

Ha!

Hester

Yr a natural! Jabber, yr little baby brothers a natural. We gonna come out on top this month, I can feel it. Try another one, Baby.

Jabber

They wrote it in yr practice place.

Hester

Yes they did.

Jabber

They wrote in yr practice place so you didnt practice today.

Hester

I practiced. In my head. In the air. In the dirt underfoot.

Jabber

Lets see.

> With great difficulty Hester makes an "A" in the dirt.

Hester

The letter A.

Jabber

Almost.

Hester

You gonna disparage me I aint gonna practice.

Baby
Mommmmieee!

Hester
Gimmieuhminute, Baby-child.

Jabber
Legs apart hands crost the chest like I showd you. Try again.

Baby
Mommieee!

Hester
See the pretty can, Baby?

Baby
Ha!

Jabber
Try again.

Baby
Mommmieee!

Hester
Later. Read that word out to me, huh? I like it when you read to me.

Jabber
Dont wanna read it.

Hester
Cant or wont?

Jabber
—Cant.

Hester
Jabber

He knows what the word says,
but he wont say it.

Hester
I was sick when I was carrying you. Damn you, slow fool.
Aaah, my treasure, cmmeer. My oldest treasure.

Hester gives him a quick hug.
She looks at the word, its letters mysterious to her.
Baby smashes can after can.

Hester
Go scrub it off, then. I like my place clean.

Jabber dutifully scrubs the wall.

Hester
We know who writ it up there. It was them bad boys writing
on my home. And in my practice place. Do they write on
they own homes? I dont think so. They come under the
bridge and write things they dont write nowhere else. A
mean ugly word, I'll bet. A word to hurt our feelings. And
because we aint lucky we gotta live with it. 5 children I got.
5 treasures. 5 joys. But we aint got our leg up, just yet. So
we gotta live with mean words and hurt feelings.

Jabber
Words dont hurt my feelings, Mamma.

Hester
Dont disagree with me.

Jabber
Sticks and stones, Mamma.

Hester
Yeah. I guess.
(Rest)
Too late for yr sisters and brother to still be out. Yr little
brother Babys gonna make us rich. He learns quick. Look at
him go.

> Hester lines up more cans and Baby jumps on them, smashing them all. Bully, her 12-year-old girl, runs in.

Bully
Mommieeeeeeeee! Mommie, Trouble he has really done it this time. I told him he was gonna be doing life and he laughed and then I said he was gonna get the electric chair and you know what he said?

Hester
Help me sack the cans.

Bully
He said a bad word!

Hester
Sack the cans.

> They sack the crushed cans.

Bully
Trouble he said something really bad but Im not saying it cause if I do yll wash my mouth. What he said was bad but what he did, what he did was worse.

Hester
Whatd he do?

Bully
Stole something.

Hester
Food?

Bully
No.

Hester
Toys?

Bully
No.

Hester

I dont like youall stealing toys and I dont like youall stealing food but it happens. I wont punish you for it. Yr just
kids. Trouble thinks with his stomach. He hungry he takes,
sees a toy, gotta have it.

Bully

A policeman saw him steal and ran after him but Trouble
ran faster cause the policeman was fat.

Hester

Policeman chased him?

Bully

He had a big stomach. Like he was pregnant. He was jig-
gling and running and yelling and red in the face.

Hester

What he steal?

Bully

—Nothing.

Hester

You talk that much and you better keep talking, Miss.

> Bully buttons her lips.
> Hester pops her upside the head.

Bully

Owwww!

Hester

Get outa my sight. Worse than a thief is a snitch that dont
snitch.

> Trouble, age 10, and Beauty, age 7, run in, breathless.
> They see Hester eyeing them and stop running;
> they walk nonchalantly.

Hester

What you got behind you?

Trouble
Nothing. Jabber, what you doing?

Jabber
Cleaning the wall.

Beauty
My hair needs a ribbon.

Hester
Not right now it dont. You steal something?

Trouble
Me? Whats cookin?

Hester
Soup of the day.

Trouble
We had soup the day yesterday.

Hester
Todays a new day.

Beauty
Is it a new soup?

Hester
Wait and see. You gonna end up in the penitentiary and embarass your mother?

Trouble
No.

Hester
If you do I'll kill you. Set the table.

Jabber
Thats girls work.

Trouble
Mommiee—

Bully

Troubles doing girls work Troubles doing girls work.

Hester

Set the damn table or Ima make a girl outa you!

Trouble

You cant make a girl outa me.

Hester

Dont push me!
(Rest)
Look, Baby. See the soup? Mommies stirring it. Dont come close, its hot.

Beauty

I want a ribbon.

Hester

Get one I'll tie it in.

> Beauty gets a ribbon.
> Trouble gets bowls, wipes them clean, hands them out.
> Hester follows behind him and,
> out of the back of his pants,
> yanks a policemans club.

Hester

Whered you get this?

Trouble
Hester
Trouble

Hester

I said—

Trouble

I found it. On the street. It was just lying there.

Bully

You stole it.

Trouble
Did not!

Hester
Dont lie to me.

Trouble
I found it. I did. It was just lying on the street. I was minding my own business.

Hester
That why the cops was chasing you?

Trouble
Snitch!

Bully
Jailbait!

> Bully hits Trouble hard.
> They fight. Pandemonium.

Hester
Suppertime!

> Order is restored.
> Hester slips the club into the belt of her dress;
> it hangs there like a sword.
> She wears it like this for most of the play.
> Her children sit in a row holding their bowls.
> She ladles out the soup.

Hester
Todays soup the day, ladies and gents, is a very special blend of herbs and spices. The broth is chef Mommies worldwide famous "whathaveyou" stock. Theres carrots in there. Theres meat. Theres oranges. Theres pie.

Trouble
What kinda pie?

Hester
What kind you like?

Trouble
Apple.

Hester
Theres apple pie.

Jabber
Pumpkin.

Bully
And cherry!

Hester
Theres pumpkin and cherry too. And steak. And mash pota-
toes for Beauty. And milk for Baby.

Beauty
And diamonds.

Jabber
You cant eat diamonds.

Hester
So when you find one in yr soup whatll you do?

Beauty
Put it on my finger.

> They slurp down their soup quickly.
> As soon as she fills their bowls, theyre empty again.
> The kids eat. Hester doesnt.

Jabber
You aint hungry?

Hester
I'll eat later.

Jabber
You always eating later.

Hester
You did a good job with the wall, Jabber. Whatd that word
say anyway?

Jabber
—Nothing.

>   The soup pot is empty.

Hester
Jabber/Bully/Trouble/Beauty/Baby

(Rest)

Hester
Bedtime.

Bully
Can we have a story?

(Rest)

Hester
All right.
(Rest)
There were once these five brothers and they were all big
and strong and handsome and didnt have a care in the
world. One was known for his brains so they called him
Smarts and one was known for his muscles, so they called
him Toughguy, the third one was a rascal so they called him
Wild, the fourth one was as goodlooking as all get out and
they called him Looker and the fifth was the youngest and
they called him Honeychild cause he was as young as he
was sweet. And they was always together these five brothers. Everywhere they went they always went together. No
matter what they was always together cause they was best
friends and wasnt nothing could divide them. And there was
this Princess. And she lived in a castle and she was lonesome. She was lonesome and looking for love but she couldnt

leave her castle so she couldnt look very far so every day she would stick her head out her window and sing to the sun and every night she would stick her head out and sing to the moon and the stars: "Where are you?" And one day the five brothers heard her and came calling and she looked upon them and she said: "There are five of you, and each one is wonderful and special in his own way. But the law of my country doesnt allow a princess to have more than one husband." And that was such bad news and they were all so in love that they all cried. Until the Princess had an idea. She was after all the Princess, so she changed the law of the land and married them all.

(Rest)

And with Bro Smarts she had a baby named Jabber. And with Bro Toughguy she had Bully. With Bro Wild came Trouble. With Bro Looker she had Beauty. With Bro Honeychild came Baby. And they was all happy.

Jabber
Until the bad news came.

Hester
No bad news came.

Jabber
Theres always bad news.

Hester
Bedtime.

Beauty
Where did the daddys go?

Hester
They went to bed.

Trouble
They ran off.

Jabber
The war came and the brothers went off to fight and they all died.

Beauty
They all died?

Jabber
And they fell into the ground and the dirt covered up they heads.

Hester
Its bedtime. Now!

Beauty
Im scared.

Trouble
I aint scared. Jabber, you a spook.

Bully
Yr the spook.

Trouble
Yr a bastard.

Bully
Yr a bastard.

Hester
Yr all bastards!

> The children burst into tears.

Hester
Cmmeer. Cmmeer. Mama loves you. Shes just tired is all. Lemmie hug you.

> They nestle around her and she hugs them.

Hester
My 5 treasures. My 5 joys.

Hester
Jabber/Bully/Trouble/Beauty/Baby
Hester

Hester

Lets hit the sack! And leave yr shoes for polish and yr shirts and blouses for press. You dont wanna look like you dont got nobody.

> They take off their shoes and tops
> and go inside leaving Hester outside alone.

Hester
Hester
Hester

(Rest)

> Hester examines the empty soup pot,
> shines the kids shoes, "presses" their clothes.
> A wave of pain shoots through her.

Hester

You didnt eat, Hester. And the pain in yr gut comes from having nothing in it.
(Rest)
Kids ate good though. Ate their soup all up. They wont starve.
(Rest)
None of these shoes shine. Never did no matter how hard you spit on em, Hester. You get a leg up the first thing you do is get shoes. New shoes for yr 5 treasures. You got yrself a good pair of shoes already.

> From underneath a pile of junk she takes a shoebox.
> Inside is a pair of white pumps.
> She looks them over then puts them away.

Hester

Dont know where yr going but yll look good when you get there.

> [Hester takes out a small tape player.
> Pops in a tape.
> She takes a piece of chalk from her pocket and,
> on the freshly scrubbed wall, practices her letters:

she writes the letter A over and over and over.
The cassette tape plays as she writes.
On tape:

Reverend D.

If you cant always do right then you got to admit that some times, some times my friends you are going to do wrong and you are going to have to *live* with that. Somehow work that into the fabric of your life. Because there aint a soul out there that is spot free. There aint a soul out there that has walked but hasnt stumbled. Aint a single solitary soul out there that has said "hello" and not "goodbye," has said "yes" to the lord and "yes" to the devil too, has drunk water and drunk wine, loved and hated, experienced the good side of the tracks and the bad. That is what they call "Livin," friends. L-I-V-I-N, friends. Life on earth is full of confusion. Life on earth is full of misunderstandings, reprimandings, and we focus on the trouble, friends, when it is the solution to those troubles we oughta be looking at. "I have fallen and I cant get up!" How many times have you heard that, friends? The fellow on the street with his whisky breath and his outstretched hand, the banker scraping the money off the top, the runaway child turned criminal all cry out "I have fallen, and I cant get up!" "I have fallen, and I cant get up!" "I have fallen—"

Hester hears someone coming and turns the tape off.]
She goes back to polishing the shoes.
Amiga Gringa comes in.

Amiga Gringa
Look at old Mother Hubbard or whatever.

Hester
Keep quiet. Theyre sleeping.

Amiga Gringa
The old woman and the shoe. Thats who you are.

Hester
I get my leg up thats what Im getting. New shoes for my treasures.

Amiga Gringa
Thatll be some leg up.

Hester
You got my money?

Amiga Gringa
Is that a way to greet a friend? "You got my money?" What world is this?

Hester
You got my money, Amiga?

Amiga Gringa
I got *news* for you, Hester. News thats better than gold. But first—heads up.

> The Doctor comes in.
> He wears a sandwich board and
> carries all his office paraphernalia on his back.

Doctor
Hester! Yr due for a checkup.

Hester
My guts been hurting me.

Doctor
Im on my way home just now. Catch up with me tomorrow. We'll have a look at it then.

> He goes on his way.

Amiga Gringa
Doc! I am in pain like you would not believe. My hips, Doc. When I move them—blinding flashes of light and then— down I go, flat on my back, like Im dead, Doc.

Doctor
I gave you something for that yesterday.

Doctor
Amiga Gringa

> He slips Amiga a few pills.
> He goes on his way.

Amiga Gringa
Hes a saint.

Hester
Sometimes.

Amiga Gringa
Want some?

Hester
I want my money.

Amiga Gringa
Patience, girl. All good things are on their way. Do you
know what the word is?

Hester
What word?

Amiga Gringa
Word is that yr first love is back in town, doing well and
looking for you.

Hester
Chilli? Jabbers daddy? Looking for me?

Amiga Gringa
Thats the word.

Hester
Hester

Hester
Bullshit. Gimmie my money, Miga. I promised the kids cake
and ice cream. How much you get?

Amiga Gringa
First, an explanation of the economic environment.

Hester
Just gimmie my money—

Amiga Gringa
The Stock Market, The Bond Market, Wall Street, Grain
Futures, Bulls and Bears and Pork Bellies. They all impact
the price a woman such as myself can get for a piece of
"found" jewelry.

Hester
That werent jewelry I gived you that was a watch. A Mans
watch. Name brand. And it was working.

Amiga Gringa
Do you know what the Dow did today, Hester? The Dow was
up twelve points. And that prize fighter, the one everyone is
talking about, the one with the pretty wife and the heavy-
weight crown, he rang the opening bell. She wore a dress
cut down to here. And the Dow shot up 43 points in the first
minutes of trading, Hester. Up like a rocket. And men
glanced up at the faces of clocks on the walls of their offices
and women around the country glanced into the faces of
their children and time passed. [And someone looks at their
watch because its lunchtime, Hester. And theyre having—
lunch. And they wish it would last forever. Cause when they
get back to their office where they—work, when they get
back the Dow has plummeted. And theres a lot of racing
around and time is brief and something must be done before
the closing bell. Phone calls are made, marriages dissolve,
promises lost in the shuffle, Hester, and all this time your
Amiga Gringa is going from fence to fence trying to get the
best price on this piece of "found" jewelry. Numbers racing
on lightboards, Hester, telling those that are in the know,
the value of who knows what. One man, broken down in
tears in the middle of the avenue, "Oh my mutual funds" he
was saying.] The market was hot, and me, a suspicious looking mother, very much like yrself, with no real address and

no valid forms of identification, walking the streets with a hot watch.
(Rest)
Here.

She gives Hester $.

Hester
Wheres the rest?

Amiga Gringa
Thats it.

Hester
5 bucks?

Amiga Gringa
It wasnt a good day. Some days are good some days are bad. I kept a buck for myself.

Hester
You stole from me.

Amiga Gringa
Dont be silly. We're friends, Hester.

Hester
I shoulda sold it myself.

Amiga Gringa
But you had the baby to watch.

Hester
And no ones gonna give money to me with me carrying Baby around. Still I coulda got more than 5.

Amiga Gringa
Go nextime yrself then. The dangers I incur, working with you. You oughta send yr kids away. Like me. I got 3 kids. All under the age of 3. And do you see me looking all baggy eyed, up all night shining little shoes and flattening little

shirts and going without food? Theres plenty of places that you can send them. Homes. Theres plenty of peoples, rich ones especially, that cant have kids. The rich spend days looking through the newspaper for ads where they can buy one. Or they go to the bastard homes and pick one out. Youd have some freedom. Youd have a chance at life. Like me.

Hester
My kids is mine. I get rid of em what do I got? Nothing.
I got nothing now, but if I lose them I got less than nothing.

Amiga Gringa
Suit yrself. You wouldnt have to send them all away, just one or two or three.

Hester
All I need is a leg up. I get my leg up I'll be ok.

>   Bully comes outside and stands there watching them.
>   She wears pink, one-piece, flame-retardant pajamas.

Hester
What.

Bully
My hands stuck.

Hester
Why you sleep with yr hands in fists?

Amiga Gringa
Yr an angry girl, arentcha, Bully.

Bully
Idunno. This ones stuck too.

Hester
Maybe yll grow up to be a boxer, huh? We can watch you ringside, huh? *Wide World of Sports*.

Amiga Gringa
Presenting in this corner weighing 82 pounds the chal-
lenger: Bully!

Bully
Ima good girl.

Hester
Course you are. There. You shouldnt sleep with yr hands
balled up. The good fairies come by in the night with treats
for little girls and they put them in yr hands. How you
gonna get any treats if yr hands are all balled up?

Bully
Jabber is bad and Trouble is bad and Beauty is bad and
Baby is bad but I'm good. Bullys a good girl.

Hester
Go on back to bed now.

Bully
Miga. Smell.

Amiga Gringa
You got bad breath.

Bully
I forgot to brush my teeth.

Hester
Go head.

> Bully squats off in the "bathroom"
> and rubs her teeth with her finger.

Amiga Gringa
Babys daddy, that Reverend, he ever give you money?

Hester
No.

Amiga Gringa
Hes a gold mine. I seen the collection plate going around. Its a full plate.

Hester
I aint seen him since before Baby was born.

Amiga Gringa
Thats two years.

Hester
He didnt want nothing to do with me. His heart went hard.

Amiga Gringa
My second kids daddy had a hard heart at first. But time mushed him up. Remember when he comed around crying about his lineage and asking whered the baby go? And I'd already gived it up.

Hester
Reverend D., his heart is real hard. Like a rock.

Amiga Gringa
Worth a try all the same.

Hester
Yeah.
(Rest)
Who told you Chilli was looking for me?

Amiga Gringa
Word on the street, thats all.

> Trouble, dressed in superhero pajamas, comes in.
> He holds a box of matches. He lights one.

Hester
What the hell you doing?

Trouble
Sleepwalking.

Hester
You sleepwalk yrself back over here and gimmie them matches or Ima kill you.

> Trouble gives her the matches.
> Bully has finished with her teeth.

Bully
You wanna smell?

Hester
Thats ok.

Bully
Dont you wanna smell?

> Hester leans in and Bully opens her mouth.

Bully
I only did one side cause I only ate with one side today.

Hester
Go on to bed.

> Bully passes Trouble and hits him hard.

Trouble
Aaaaah!

Bully
Yr a bad person!

> Bully hits him again.

Trouble
Aaaaaaaaah!

Hester
Who made you policewoman?

Trouble
Ima blow you sky high one day you bully bitch!

> Bully goes to hit him again.

Hester

Trouble I thought you said you was sleep. Go inside and lie
down and shut up or you wont see tomorrow.

> Trouble goes back to sleepwalking and goes inside.

Hester

Bully. Go over there. Close yr eyes and yr mouth and not a
word, hear?

> Bully goes a distance off
> curling up to sleep without a word.

Hester

I used to wash Troubles mouth out with soap when he used
bad words. Found out he likes the taste of soap. Sometimes
you cant win. No matter what you do.
(Rest)
Im gonna talk to Welfare and get an upgrade. The worldll
take care of the women and children.

Amiga Gringa

Theyre gonna give you the test. See what skills you got.
Make you write stuff.

Hester

Like what?

Amiga Gringa

Like yr name.

Hester

I can write my damn name. Im not such a fool that I cant
write my own goddamn name. I can write my goddamn
name.

> Inside, Baby starts crying.

Hester

HUSH!

Baby hushes.

Amiga Gringa
You should pay yrself a visit to Babys daddy. Dont take
along the kid in the flesh thatll be too much. For a buck I'll
get someone to take a snapshot.

> Jabber comes in. He wears mismatched pajamas.
> He doesnt come too close, keeps his distance.

Jabber
I was in a rowboat and the sea was flat like a blue plate and
you was rowing me and it was fun.

Hester
Go back to bed.

Jabber
It was a good day but then Bad News and the sea started
rolling and the boat tipped and I fell out and—

Hester
You wet the bed.

Jabber
I fell out the boat.

Hester
You wet the bed.

Jabber
I wet the bed.

Hester
13 years old still peeing in the bed.

Jabber
It was uh accident.

Hester
Whats wrong with you?

Jabber
Accidents happen.

Hester
Yeah you should know cause yr uh damn accident. Shit.
Take that off.

Jabber strips.

Amiga Gringa
He aint bad looking, Hester. A little slow, but some women
like that.

Hester
Wear my coat. Gimmie a kiss.

Jabber puts on Hesters coat and kisses her on the cheek.

Jabber
Mommie?

Hester
Bed.

Jabber
All our daddys died, right? All our daddys died in the war,
right?

Hester
Yeah, Jabber.

Jabber
They went to war and they died and you cried. They went to
war and died but whered they go when they died?

Hester
They into other things now.

Jabber
Like what?

Hester

—. Worms. They all turned into worms, honey. They crawling around in the dirt happy as larks, eating the world up, never hungry. Go to bed.

Jabber goes in.

(Rest)

Amiga Gringa
Worms?

Hester
Whatever.

Amiga Gringa
Hes yr favorite. You like him the best.

Hester
Hes my first.

Amiga Gringa
Hes yr favorite.

Hester
I dont got no *favorite.*
(Rest)
5 bucks. 3 for their treats. And one for that photo. Reverend D. aint the man I knew. Hes got money now. A salvation business and all. Maybe his stone-heart is mush, though. Maybe.

Amiga Gringa
Cant hurt to try.

SCENE 2
Street Practice

> Hester walks alone down the street.
> She has a framed picture of Baby.

Hester
Picture, it comed out pretty good. Got him sitting on a chair,
and dont he look like he got everything one could want in
life? Hes 2 years old. Andll be growd up with a life of his
own before I blink.
(Rest)
Picture comed out good. Thought Amiga was cheating me
but it comed out good.

> Hester meets the Doctor, coming the other way.
> As before he carries all of his office paraphernalia
> on his back. He wears a sandwich board,
> the words written on it are hidden.

Doctor
Hester. Dont move a muscle, I'll be set up in a jiffy.

Hester
I dont got more than a minute.

Doctor
Hows yr gut?

Hester
Not great.

Doctor
Say "Aaaah!"

Hester
Aaaah!

> As Hester stands there with her mouth open,
> he sets up his roadside office: a thin curtain,
> his doctors shingle, his instruments, his black bag.

Doctor
Good good good good good. Lets take yr temperature. Do
you know what it takes to keep my road-side practice running? Do you know how much The Higher Ups would like to
shut me down? Every blemish on your record is a blemish
on mine. Take yr guts for instance. Yr pain could be nothing
or it could be the end of the road—a cyst or a tumor, a lump
or a virus or an infected sore. Or cancer, Hester. Undetected.
There youd be, lying in yr coffin with all yr little ones
gathered around motherlessly weeping and The Higher
Ups pointing their fingers at me, saying I should of saved
the day, but instead stood idly by. You and yr children live
as you please and Im the one The Higher Ups hold
responsible. Would you like a pill?

Hester
No thanks.

> Hester doubles over in pain.

Hester
My gut hurts.

> The Doctor takes a pill.

Doctor
In a minute. We'll get to that in a minute. How are yr children?

Hester
Theyre all right.

Doctor
All 5?

Hester
All 5.

Doctor
Havent had any more have you?

Hester
No.

Doctor
But you could. But you might.

Hester
—Maybe.

Doctor
Word from The Higher Ups is that one more kid outa the
likes of you and theyre on the likes of me like white on rice.
I'd like to propose something—. Yr running a temperature.
Bit of a fever. Whats this?

Hester
Its a club. For protection.

Doctor
Good thinking.

> The Doctor examines her quickly and thoroughly.

Doctor
The Higher Ups are breathing down my back, Hester. They
want answers! They want results! Solutions! Solutions!
Solutions! Thats what they want.

> He goes to take another pill, but doesnt.

Doctor
I only take one a day. I only allow myself one a day.
(Rest)

Doctor
Breathe in deep. Lungs are clear. Yr heart sounds good.
Strong as an ox.

Hester
This falls been cold. The wind under the bridge is colder
than the wind on the streets.

Doctor
Exercise. Thats what I suggest. When the temperature
drops, I run in place. Hold yr hands out. Shaky.
Experiencing any stress and tension?

Hester
Not really.

Doctor
Howre yr meals?

Hester
The kids come first.

Doctor
Course they do. Howre yr bowels. Regular?

Hester
I dunno.

Doctor
Once a day?

Hester
Sometimes. My gut—

Doctor
In a minute. Gimmie the Spread & Squat right quick. Lets
have a look under the hood.

> Standing, Hester spreads her legs and squats.
> Like an otter, he slides between her legs on a dolly
> and looks up into her privates with a flashlight.

Doctor
Last sexual encounter?

Hester
Thats been a while, now.

Doctor
Yve healed up well from yr last birth.

Hester
Its been 2 years. His names Baby.

Doctor
Any pain, swelling, off-color discharge, strange smells?

Hester
No.

Doctor
L.M.P.?

Hester
About a week ago.
(Rest)
How *you* been feeling, Doc?

Doctor
Sometimes Im up, sometimes Im down.

Hester
You said you was lonesome once. I came for a checkup and
you said you was lonesome. You lonesome today, Doc?

Doctor
No.

Hester
Oh.

　　Far away, Chilli walks by with his picnic basket on his arm.
　　He pauses, checks his pocket watch, then continues on.

Doctor
Yr intelligent. Attractive enough. You could of made something of yrself.

Hester
Im doing all right.

Doctor
The Higher Ups say yr in a skid. I agree.

Hester
Oh, I coulda been the Queen of Sheba, it just werent in the cards, Doc.

Doctor
Yr kids are 5 strikes against you.

Hester
I dont need no lecture. Gimmie something for my gut so I can go.

Doctor
The Higher Ups, they say Im not making an impact. But what do you care.

Hester
My gut—

Doctor
Stand right here.

> The Doctor draws a line in the dirt, positions her
> behind it and walks a few steps away. He reveals
> the writing on his sandwich board. It is an eye exam chart.
> The letters on the first line spell "SPAY."

Doctor
Read.

Hester
—. A.

Doctor
Good.

> He takes a step closer decreasing the
> distance between them.

Doctor
Read.

Hester
—. —. —.
(Rest)
I need glasses for that.

Doctor
Uh huhn.

> He steps closer.

Doctor
How about now?

Hester
I need glasses I guess.

Doctor
I guess you do.

> He steps even closer.

Hester
((somethin-somethin-A-somethin.))
(Rest)
I need glasses.

Doctor
You cant read this?

Hester
I gotta go.

Doctor

When I say removal of your "womanly parts" do you know what parts Im talking about?

Hester

Yr gonna take my womans parts?

Doctor

My hands are tied. The Higher Ups are calling the shots now.
(Rest)
You have 5 healthy children, itll be for the best, considering.

Hester

My womans parts.

Doctor

Ive fowarded my recommendation to yr caseworker. Its out of my hands. Im sorry.

Hester

I gotta go.

But she doesnt move.
She stands there numbly.

Doctor

Yr gut. Lets have a listen.

He puts his ear to her stomach and listens.

Doctor

Growling hungry stomach. Heres a dollar. Go get yrself a sandwich.

Hester takes the money and goes.

Doctor
Doctor
Doctor

FIRST CONFESSION: THE DOCTOR
"Times Are Tough: What Can We Do?"

Doctor
Times are tough:
What can we do?
When I see a woman begging on the streets I guess I could
bring her in my house
sit her at my table
make her a member of my family, sure.
But there are hundreds and thousands of them
and my house cant hold them all.
Maybe we should all take in just one.
Except they wouldnt really fit.
They wouldnt really fit in with us.
Theres such a gulf between us. What can we do?
I am a man of the people, from way back my streetside practice
is a testement to that
so dont get me wrong
do not for a moment think that I am one of those people haters
     who does not understand who does not experience—
     compassion.
(Rest)
Shes been one of my neediest cases for several years now.
What can I do?
Each time she comes to me
looking more and more forlorn
and more and more in need
of affection.
At first I wouldnt touch her without gloves on, but then—
(Rest)
we did it once
in that alley there,
she was
phenomenal.
(Rest)
I was
lonesome and
she gave herself to me in a way that I had never experienced
even with women Ive paid

she was, like she was giving me something that was not hers
    to give me but something that was mine
that I'd lent her
and she was returning it to me.
Sucked me off for what seemed like hours
but I was very insistent. And held back
and she understood that I wanted her in the traditional way.
And she was very giving very motherly very obliging very
    understanding
very phenomenal.
Let me cumm inside her. Like I needed to.
What could I do?
I couldnt help it.

SCENE 3
The Reverend on His Soapbox

> Late at night. The Reverend D.
> on his soapbox preaching to no one in particular.
> There are audio recordings of his sermons for sale.

Reverend D.
You all know me. You all know this face. These arms. These
legs. This body of mine is known to you. To all of you. There
isnt a person on the street tonight that hasnt passed me by
at some point. Maybe when I was low, many years ago, with
a bottle in my hand and the cold hard unforgiving pavement
for my dwelling place. Perhaps you know me from that.
Or perhaps you know me from my more recent incarnation.
The man on the soapbox, telling you of a better life thats
available to you, not after the demise of your physical being,
not in some heaven where we all gonna be robed in satin
sheets and wearing gossamer wings, but right here on earth,
my friends. Right here right now. Let the man on the soapbox
tell you how to pick yourself up. Let the man on the soapbox
tell you how all yr dreams can come true. Let the man on
the soapbox tell you that you dont have to be down and
dirty, you dont have to be ripped off and renounced, you
dont have to be black and blue, your neck dont have to be
red, your clothes dont have to be torn, your head dont have
to be hanging, you dont have to *hate* yourself, you dont have
to hate yr neighbor. You can pull yrself up.

> Hester comes in with a framed picture of Baby.
> She stands a ways off. Reverend D. keeps on talking.

Reverend D.
And I am an example of that. I am a man who has crawled
out of the quicksand of despair. I am a man who has pulled
himself out of that never ending gutter—and you notice
friends that every city and every towns got a gutter. Aint no
place in the world that dont have some little trench for its
waste. And the gutter, is endless, and deep and wide and if
you think you gonna crawl out of the gutter by crawling
along the gutter you gonna be in the gutter for the rest of
your life. You gotta step out of it, friends and I am here to
tell you that you can.

(Rest)

> He sees Hester but doesnt recognize her.

Reverend D.
What can I do for you tonight, my sister.

Hester
I been good.

Reverend D.
But yr life is weighing heavy on you tonight.

Hester
I havent bothered you.

Reverend D.
Reverend D. likes to be bothered. Reverend D. enjoys having the tired, the deprived and the depraved come knocking
on his door. Come gathering around his soapbox. Come
closer. Come on.

> Hester holds the picture of Baby in front of her face,
> hiding her face from view.

Hester
This child here dont know his daddy.

Reverend D.
The ultimate disaster of modern times. Sweet child. Yours?

Hester
Yes.

Reverend D.
Do you know the father?

Hester
Yes.

Reverend D.
You must go to him and say, "Mister, here is your child!"

Hester
Mister here is your child!

Reverend D.
"You are wrong to deny what God has made!"

Hester
You are wrong to deny what God has made!

Reverend D.
"He has nothing but love for you and reaches out his hands every day crying wheres daddy?"

Hester
Wheres daddy?

Reverend D.
"Wont you answer those cries?"

Hester
Wont you answer those cries?

Reverend D.
If he dont respond to that then hes a good-for-nothing dead-beat, and you report him to the authorities. Theyll garnish his wages so at least you all wont starve. I have a motivational cassette which speaks to that very subject. I'll give it to you free of charge.

Hester

I got all yr tapes. I send my eldest up here to get them.

Reverend D.

Wonderful. Thats wonderful. You should go to yr childs father and demand to be recognized.

Hester

Its been years since I seen him. He didnt want me bothering him so I been good.

Reverend D.

Go to him. Plead with him. Show him this sweet face and yours. He cannot deny you.

> Hester lowers the picture, revealing her face.

Hester
Reverend D.
Hester
Reverend D.

(Rest)

Hester

You know me?

Reverend D.

No. God.

Hester

I aint bothered you for 2 years.

Reverend D.

You should go. Home. Let me call you a taxi. *Taxi!* You shouldnt be out this time of night. Young mother like you. In a neighborhood like this. We'll get you home in a jiff. Where ya live? East? West? North I bet, am I right? *TAXI!* God.

Hester

hes talking now. Not much but some. hes a good boy.

Reverend D.

I am going to send one of my people over to your home tomorrow. Theyre marvelous, the people who work with me. Theyll put you in touch with all sorts of agencies that can help you. Get some food in that stomach of yours. Get you some sleep.

Hester

Doctor says I got a fever. We aint doing so good. We been slipping. I been good. I dont complain. They breaking my back is all. 5 kids. My treasures, breaking my back.

Reverend D.

We'll take up a collection for you.

Hester

You know me.

Reverend D.

You are under the impression that—. Your mind, having nothing better to fix itself on, has fixed on me. Me, someone youve never even met.

Hester

There aint no one here but you and me. Say it. You know me. You know my name. You know my—. You know me and I know you.

Hester
Reverend D.

(Rest)

Reverend D.

Here is a card. My lawyer. He'll call you.

Hester

We dont got no phone.

Reverend D.

He'll visit. Write yr address on—. Tell me yr address. I'll

write it down. I'll give it to him in the morning and he'll visit you.
(Rest)
Do the authorities know the name of the father?

Hester
I dont tell them nothing.

Reverend D.
They would garnish his wages if you did. That would provide you with a small income. If you agree not to ever notify the authorities, we could, through my instutition, arrange for you to get a much larger amount of money.

Hester
How much more?

Reverend D.
Twice as much.

Hester
3 times.

Reverend D.
Fine.

Hester
Theres so many things we need. Food. New shoes. A regular dinner with meat and salad and bread.

Reverend D.
I should give you some money right now. As a promise to you that I'll keep my word. But Im short of cash.

Hester
Oh.

Reverend D.
Come back in 2 days. Late. I'll have some then.

Hester
You dont got no food or nothing do ya?

Reverend D.
Come back in 2 days. Not early. Late. And not a word to no
one. Okay?

Hester
—. K.

Reverend D.
Hester
Reverend D.
Hester

(Rest)

Reverend D.
You better go.

Hester goes.

SCENE 4
With the Welfare

Outside, Jabber, Trouble and Beauty
sit in the dirt playing with toy cars.

Trouble
Red light. Greet light. Red light. Green light.

Jabber
Look, a worm.

They all study the worm as it
writhes in the dirt. Welfare enters.

Welfare
Wheres your mommie?

Beauty
Inside.

Jabber
Mommie! Welfares here.

Welfare
Thank you.

Hester
You all go inside.

In the Blood **53**

The kids go inside.

Welfare
Hands clean?

Hester
Yes, Maam.

Welfare
Wash them again.

Hester washes her hands again.
Dries them.

Welfare
The welfare of the world.

Hester
Maam?

Welfare
Come on over, come on.

Hester stands behind Welfare,
giving her a shoulder rub.

Welfare
The welfare of the world weighs on these shoulders, Hester.
(Rest)
We at Welfare are at the end of our rope with you. We put
you in a job and you quit. We put you in a shelter and you
walk. We put you in school and you drop out. Yr children
are also truant. Word is they steal. Stealing is a gateway
crime, Hester. Perhaps your young daughter is pregnant.
Who knows. We build bridges you burn them. We sew safety
nets, rub harder, good strong safety nets and you slip
through the weave.

Hester
We was getting by all right, then I dunno, I been tired lately.
Like something in me broke.

Welfare

You and yr children live, who knows where.

Hester

Here, Maam, under the Main Bridge.

Welfare

This is not the country, Hester. You cannot simply—live off the land. If yr hungry you go to the shelter and get a hot meal.

Hester

The shelter hassles me. Always prying in my business. Stealing my shit. Touching my kids. We was making ends meet all right then—ends got further apart.

Welfare

"Ends got further apart." God!
(Rest)
I care because it is my job to care. I am paid to stretch out these hands, Hester. Stretch out these hands. To you.

Hester

I gived you the names of 4 daddys: Jabbers and Bullys and Troubles and Beautys. You was gonna find them. Garnish they wages.

Welfare

No luck as yet but we're looking. Sometimes these searches take years.

Hester

Its been years.

Welfare

Lifetimes then. Sometimes they take that long. These men of yours, theyre deadbeats. They dont want to be found. Theyre probably all in Mexico wearing false mustaches. Ha ha ha.
(Rest)
What about the newest child?

Hester
Baby.

Welfare
What about "Babys" father?

Hester
—. I dunno.

Welfare
Dont know or dont remember?

Hester
You think Im doing it with mens I dont know?

Welfare
No need to raise your voice no need of that at all. You have
to help me help you, Hester.
(Rest)
Run yr fingers through my hair. Go on. Feel it. Silky isnt it?

Hester
Yes, Maam.

Welfare
Comes from a balanced diet. Three meals a day. Strict
adherence to the food pyramid. Money in my pocket,
clothes on my back, teeth in my mouth, womanly parts
where they should be, hair on my head, husband in my bed.

> Hester combs Welfares hair.

Welfare
Yr doctor recommends that you get a hysterectomy. Take out
yr womans parts. A spay.

Hester
Spay.

Welfare
I hope things wont come to that. I will do what I can. But
you have to help me, Hester.

Hester
((Dont *make* me hurt you.))

Welfare
What?

Hester
I didnt mean it. Just slipped out.

Welfare
Remember yr manners. We worked good and hard on yr
manners. Remember? Remember that afternoon over at my
house? That afternoon with the teacups?

Hester
Manners, Maam?

Welfare
Yes. Manners.

Hester
Welfare

Welfare
Babys daddy. Whats his name?

Hester
You wont find him no how.

Welfare
We could get lucky. He could be right around the corner
and I could walk out and there he would be and then we at
Welfare would wrestle him to the ground and turn him
upside down and let you and yr Baby grab all the money
that falls from Deadbeat Daddys pockets. I speak metaphor-
ically. We would garnish his wages.

Hester
How much would that put in my pocket?

Welfare
Depends how much he earns. Maybe 100. Maybe. We take
our finders fee. Whats his name?

Hester
I dunno.

Welfare
You dont have to say it out loud. Write it down.

> She gives Hester pencil and paper.
> Hester writes. Welfare looks at the paper.

Welfare
"A."
(Rest)
Adam, Andrew, Archie, Arthur, Aloysius, "A" what?

Hester
Looks good dont it?

Welfare
You havent learned yr letters yet, have you?

Hester
I want my leg up is all.

Welfare
You wont get something for nothing.

Hester
I been good.

Welfare
5 bastards is not good. 5 bastards is bad.

Hester
Dont make me hurt you!

> Hester raises her club to strike Welfare.

Welfare

You hurt me and, kids or no kids, I'll have you locked up.
We'll take yr kids away and yll never see them again.

Hester

My lifes my own fault. I know that. But the world dont help,
Maam.

Welfare

The world is not here to help us, Hester. The world is simply here. We must help ourselves.
(Rest)
I know just the job for you. It doesnt pay well, but the work
is very rewarding. Hard honest work. Unless yr afraid of
hard honest work.

Hester

I aint afraid of hard work.

Welfare

Its sewing. You can do it at home. No work no pay but thats
yr decision.
(Rest)
Heres the fabric. Make sure you dont get it dirty.

Hester

Can I express myself?

Welfare

Needles, thread and the pattern, in this bag. Take the cloth.
Sew it. If you do a good job therell be more work. Have it
sewn by tomorrow morning, yll get a bonus.

> Hester takes the cloth and notions.

Hester

I dont think the world likes women much.

Welfare

Dont be silly.

Hester

I was just thinking.

Welfare
Im a woman too! And a black woman too just like you. Dont
be silly.

Hester
Welfare

(Rest)

> Hester puts her hand out, waiting.

Hester
Yr shoulders. Plus I did yr hair.

Welfare
Is a buck all right?

Hester
Welfare

Welfare
Unless yll change a 50.

Hester
I could go get change—

Welfare
Take the buck, K? And the cloth. And go.

> Welfare owes Hester more $,
> but after a beat, Hester just leaves.

SECOND CONFESSION: THE WELFARE
"I Walk the Line"

Welfare
I walk the line
between us and them
between our kind and their kind.

The balance of the system depends on a well-drawn
     boundary line
and all parties respecting that boundary.
I am
I am a married woman.
I dont—that is have never
never in the past or even in the recent present or even when
     I look
look out into the future of my life I do not see any interest
any *sexual* interest
in anyone
other than my husband.
(Rest)
My dear husband.
The hours he keeps.
The money he brings home.
Our wonderful children.
The vacations we go on.
My dear husband he needed
a little spice.
And I agreed. We both needed spice.
We both hold very demanding jobs.
We put an ad in the paper: "Husband and Bi-Curious Wife,
     seeking—"
But the women we got:
Hookers. Neurotics. Gold diggers!
"Bring one of those gals home from work," Hubby said. And
Hester,
she came to tea.
(Rest)
She came over and we had tea.
From my mothers china.
And marzipan on matching china plates.
Hubby sat opposite in the recliner
hard as Gibralter. He told us what he wanted and we did it.
We were his little puppets.
She was surprised, but consented.
Her body is better than mine.
Not a single stretchmark on her.
Im a looker too dont get me wrong just in a different way and
Hubby liked the contrast.

Just light petting at first.
Running our hands on each other
then Hubby joined in
and while she and I kissed
Hubby did her and me alternately.
The thrill of it—.
(Rest)
I was so afraid I'd catch something
but I was swept away and couldnt stop.
She stuck her tongue down my throat
and Hubby doing his thing on top
my skin shivered.
She let me slap her across the face
and I crossed the line.
(Rest)
It was my first threesome
and it wont happen again.
And I should emphasize that
she is a low-class person.
What I mean by that is that we have absolutely nothing in
    common.
As her caseworker I realize that maintenance of the system
    depends on a well-drawn boundary line
and all parties respecting that boundary.
And I am, after all,
I am a married woman.

> Welfare exits.
> Hester reenters, watches Welfare exit.

Hester
Bitch.

> Hester, alone on stage,
> examines the cloth Welfare gave her.

Hester
Sure is pretty cloth. Sewing cant be that hard. Thread the
needle stick it in and pull it through. Pretty cloth. Lets see
what we making. Oooooh. Uh evening dress. Go to a party
in. Drink champagne and shit. Uh huh, "Dont mind if I do,"

and shit and la de *dah* and come up in a limo and every-
body wants a picture. So many lights Im blinded. Wear dark
glasses. Strut my stuff.

> Hester has another painful stomach attack
> which knocks the wind out of her and doubles her over.
> Far away, Chilli walks by with his picnic basket on his arm.
> He pauses, checks his pocket watch, then continues on.
> Hester, recovering from her attack,
> sees him just before he disappears.

Hester
Chilli!

> Intermission

SCENE 5
Small Change and Sandwiches

> Late at night. The children inside, all sleeping.
> Lots of "A's" written in Hesters practice place.
> Hester, working on her sewing,
> tries to thread the needle.

Hester
Damn needle eyes too damn small. Howmy supposed to get
the thread through. Theres a catch to everything, Hester. No
easy money nowheres. Wet the thread good. Damn.

> She squeezes her eyes shut and opens them,
> trying to focus. Having difficulty threading the needle,
> she takes out an object wrapped in brown paper.
> Looks cautiously around. Begins to unwrap it.
> A sandwich.

Hester
Put something in my stomach maybe my eyesll work.

> Amiga Gringa comes in.
> Hester stashes the package, picks up her sewing.

Amiga Gringa
Mother Hubbard sewing by street lamp. Very moving.

Hester
I got me uh job. This here is work.

Amiga Gringa
From Welfare?

Hester
Shes getting me back in the workforce. I do good on this she'll give me more.

Amiga Gringa
Whats the pay?

Hester
Its by the piece.

Amiga Gringa
How much?

Hester
10 bucks maybe.

Amiga Gringa
Maybe?

Hester
I get a bonus for working fast.

Amiga Gringa
Very nice fabric. Very pretty. Very expensive. And oooh, look at what yr making.

Hester
You good with needles? Thread this. My eyes aint good.

  Amiga tries halfheartedly to thread the needle. Quits.

Amiga Gringa
Sorry.

  Hester continues trying to thread the needle.

Hester
Today we had uh E-clipse. You seen it?

Amiga Gringa
Cant say I did. Good yr working. Getting some money in yr pocket. Making a good example for the kids. Pulling yrself up by yr bootstraps. Getting with the program. Taking responsibility for yr life. I envy you.

Hester
Me?

Amiga Gringa
Yr working, Im—looking for work.

Hester
I bet I could get you some sewing.

Amiga Gringa
Oh no. Thats not for me. If I work, Hester, I would want to be paid a living wage. You have agreed to work for less than a living wage. May as well be a slave. Or an animal.

Hester
Its a start. She said if I do well—

Amiga Gringa
If you do well shes gonna let you be her slave *for life*. Wouldnt catch me doing that. Chump work. No no no. But its a good thing you are. Example to the kids.

Hester
I aint no chump.

Amiga Gringa
Course you arent. Yr just doing chump work is all.

Hester
Its a leg up. Cant start from the top.

Amiga Gringa
Why not? Plenty of people start from the top. Why not you? Sure is pretty fabric.

Hester
All I gotta do is sew along the lines.

Amiga Gringa
Bet the fabric cost a lot. I wonder how much we could get for it—on the open market.

Hester
Aint mine to sell. Its gonna make a nice dress. Im gonna sew it up and try it on before I give it to her. Just for fun.

> But Hester still hasnt been able to thread the needle.

Amiga Gringa
Bet we could get 100 bucks. For the fabric. A lot more than youd get for sewing it. And you wouldnt have to lift a finger. I'd sell it tonight. Have the money for you in the morning.

Hester
No thanks.

Amiga Gringa
Suit yrself.

> Hester continues trying to thread that damn needle.

Amiga Gringa
Chump work.

Hester
They make the eyes too small, thats the problem.
(Rest)
I seen Chilli right after I was with the Welfare. You said he was looking for me and there he was! Jabbers daddy walking right by with a big gold pocket watch. But did I tell? Did I run after Welfare and say, "Theres Jabbers daddy?" I did not. Can you imagine?

Amiga Gringa
I told ya he was looking for ya. Hes gonna find you too.

Hester
Jabbers daddy, after all these years!

Amiga Gringa
Maybe yr lucks turning.

Hester
You think?

Amiga Gringa
Maybe.

Amiga Gringa
Hester

(Rest)

Amiga Gringa
I missed my period.

Hester
Dont look at *me*.
(Rest)
Whatcha gonna do.

Amiga Gringa
Have it, I guess.

Hester
You may not be knocked up.

Amiga Gringa
Theres something in here all right. I can feel it growing
inside. Just my luck.

Hester
You shoulda been careful.

Amiga Gringa
—Whatever.

Hester
So get rid of it if you dont want it.

Amiga Gringa
Or birth it then sell it.

Hester
You as crazy as they come.

Amiga Gringa
Hester
Amiga Gringa

> Amiga leans toward Hester to kiss her.
> Hester pulls back a bit.

Amiga Gringa
Whassamatter?

Hester
I dont got no love for nobody cept the kids.

> Amiga pulls back, takes up the fabric.

Amiga Gringa
I'll get you a lot of money for this.

Hester
No.

Amiga Gringa
Whassis?

> Amiga Gringa discovers the brown paper package.

Hester
Nothing.

Amiga Gringa
Smells like something. Smells like food. Smells like egg salad.

Hester

I was saving it.

Amiga Gringa

Lets celebrate! Come on itll be fun. Kids!

Hester

They *sleep*. Let em sleep.

Amiga Gringa

Lets toast my new kid. Just you and me. A new life has
begun. Am I showing? Not yet, right? Will be soon enough.
Little Bastards in there living high on the hog, taking up
space. Little Bastard, we toast you with: egg salad.

> Amiga takes a big bite out of the sandwich.
> Hester grabs at it but Amiga keeps it from her reach.
> Bully comes outside.

Bully

Mommie?

Hester

Yes, Bully.

Bully

My hands.

Hester

Lemmie unlock em.

> Bully comes over. Hester opens her hands.

Bully

Egg salad?

Amiga Gringa

Yeah. Its yr mommies sandwich.

> Amiga gives the sandwich to Hester
> who almost takes a bite but sees Bully looking on hungrily.

Hester
Cheat me and I'll kill you.

Amiga Gringa
Have a little faith, Hester. Amiga will sell this fabric for
you. You will not be a chump. In the morning when the sun
comes up yll be 100 bucks richer. Sleep tight.

Amiga takes the fabric and leaves.
Bully sits with her mother, licking her fingers.

THIRD CONFESSION: AMIGA GRINGA
"In My Head I Got It Going On"

Amiga Gringa
In my head I got it going on.
The triple X rated movie:
Hester and Amiga get down and get dirty.
Chocolate and Vanilla get into the ugly.
We coulda done a sex show behind a curtain
then make a movie and sell it
for 3 bucks a peek.
I had me some delicious schemes
to get her out of that hole she calls home.
Im doing well for myself
working my money maker.
Do you have any idea how much cash I'll get for the fruit of
    my white womb?!
Grow it.
Birth it.
Sell it.
And why shouldnt I?
(Rest)
Funny how a woman like Hester
driving her life all over the road
most often chooses to walk the straight and narrow.

Girl on girl action is a very lucrative business.
And someones gotta do something for her.
Im just trying to help her out.
And myself too, ok. They dont call it Capitalizm for nothing.
(Rest)
She liked the idea of the sex
at least she acted like it.
Her looking at me with those eyes of hers.
You looking like you want it, Hester.
Shoot, Miga, she says thats just the way I look she says.
It took a little cajoling to get her to do it with me
for an invited audience.
For a dime a look.
Over at my place.
Every cent was profit and no overhead to speak of.
The guys in the neighborhood got their pleasure
and we was our own boss so we didnt have to pay no joker
    off the top.
We slipped right into a very profitable situation
like sliding into warm water.
Her breasts her bottom
she let me touch her however I wanted
I let her ride my knees.
She made sounds like an animal.
She put her hand between my legs.
One day some of the guys took advantage.
Ah, what do you expect in a society based on Capitalizm.
I tell you the plight of the worker these days—.
Still one day Im gonna get her to make the movie
cause her and me we had the moves down
very sensual, very provocative, very scientific, very lucrative.
In my head I got it going on.

SCENE 6
The Reverend on the Rock

Late at night. Down the road, Reverend D. cleaning his
cornerstone, a white block of granite bearing the date
in Roman numerals, and practicing his preaching.

[**Reverend D.**
"It is easier for a camel to go through the eye of a needle
than for a rich man to enter the kingdom of God." And you
hear that and you say, let me get a tax shelter and hide some
of my riches so that when I stand up there in judgment God
wont be none the wiser! And that is the problem with the
way we see God. For most of us, God is like the IRS. God
garnishes yr wages if you dont pay up. God withholds. The
wages of sin, they lead to death, so you say, let me give to
the poor. But not any poor, just those respectable charities.
I want my poor looking good. I want my poor to know that it
was me who bought the such and such. I want my poor on tv.
I want famous poor, not miscellaneous poor. And I dont
want local poor. Local poor dont look good. Gimmie foreign
poor. Poverty exotica. Gimmie brown and yellow skins
against a non-Western landscape, some savanna, some rain
forest some rice paddy. Gimmie big sad eyes with the berri-
berri belly and the outstretched hands struggling to say
"Thank You" the only english they know, right into the camera.
And put me up there with them, holding them, comforting
them, telling them everythings gonna be alright, we gonna
raise you up, we gonna get you on the bandwagon of our ways,
put a smile in yr heart and a hamburger in yr belly, baby.
(Rest)

And that is how we like our poor. At arms length. Like a distant relation with no complication. But folks, we gotta—]

> Hester comes in and watches him.
> After a while, he notices her and stops talking.

Hester
Nice rock.

Reverend D.
Thank you.

Hester
Theres writing on it.

Reverend D.
Dont come close. Its the date its just the date. The date. Well, the year.

Hester
Like a calendar.

Reverend D.
Its a cornerstone. The first stone of my new church. My backers are building me a church and this is the first stone.

Hester
Oh.
(Rest)
You told me to come back. Im back.

Reverend D.
Theyll start building my church tomorrow. My church will be a beautiful place. Its not much of a neighborhood now but when my church gets built, oh therell be a turnaround. Lots of opportunity for everyone. I feel like one of the pilgrims. You know, they step out of their boats and on to that Plymouth rock. I step off my soapbox and on to my cornerstone.

Hester
You said come back to get my money. Im back.

Reverend D.
Do you know what a "backer" is?

Hester
Uh-uhn.

Reverend D.
Its a person who backs you. A person who believes in you.
A person who looks you over and figures you just might
make something of yrself. And they get behind you. With
kind words, connections to high places, money. But they
want to make sure they havent been suckered, so they
watch you real close, to make sure yr as good as they think
you are. To make sure you wont screw up and shame them
and waste their money.
(Rest)
My backers are building me a church. It will be beautiful.
And to make sure theyre not wasting their money on a man
who was only recently a neerdowell, they watch me.

Hester
They watching now?

Reverend D.
Not now. Now theyre in their nice beds. Between the cool
sheets. Fast asleep. I dont sleep. I have this feeling that if I
sleep I will miss someone. Someone in desperate need of
what I have to say.

Hester
Someone like me.

Reverend D.
I dont have your money yet but I will. I'll take up a collection for you on Sunday. I'll tell them yr story, that yr someone in need, and all the money will go to you. Every cent of
it. We get good crowds on Sunday.
(Rest)
Ive got work to do.

> He waits for her to go but she stays.
> He goes back to cleaning his cornerstone.

Hester
Today we had uh *E*-clipse. You seen it?

Reverend D.
You should go.

Hester
A shadow passed over the sky. Everything was dark. For a minute.

Reverend D.
It was a cloud. Or an airplane. Happens all the time.

Hester
No clouds out today. It was uh *E*-clipse.

Reverend D.
I am taking a collection for you on Sunday. Youll have to wait until then. Good night.

Hester
Uh *E*-clipse.

Reverend D.
There was no eclipse today! No eclipse!
(Rest)
Good night.

Hester
I was crossing the street with the kids. We had a walk sign. White is walk and red is dont walk. I know white from red. Aint colorblind, right? And we was crossing. And a shadow fell over, everything started going dark and, shoot I had to look up. They say when theres uh *E*-clipse you shouldnt look up cause then you go blind and alls I need is to go blind, thank you. But I couldnt help myself. And so I stopped right there in the street and looked up. Never seen nothing like it.
(Rest)
I dont know what I expected to see but.
(Rest)

It was a big dark thing. Blocking the sun out. Like the hand of fate. The hand of fate with its 5 fingers coming down on me.
(Rest)
(Rest)
And then the trumpets started blaring.
(Rest)
And then there was Jabber saying "Come on Mommie, Come on!" The trumpets was the taxi cabs. Wanting to run me over. Get out the road.

Reverend D.
Hester
Reverend D.
Hester

Reverend D. sits on his rock, his back hiding his behavior which has become unseemly.

Reverend D.
Comeer.

Hester slowly goes to him.

Reverend D.
Suck me off.

Hester
No.

Reverend D.
Itll only take a minute. Im halfway there. Please.

She goes down on him. Briefly. He cumms. Mildly. Into his handkerchief. She stands there. Ashamed. Expectant.

Reverend D.
Go home. Put yr children to bed.

Hester
Maybe we could get something regular going again—

Reverend D.
Go home. Go home.

Hester
Reverend D.

(Rest)

Reverend D.
Heres something. Its all I have.

> He offers her a crumpled bill which she takes.

Reverend D.
Next time you come by—. It would be better if you could
come around to the *back*. My churchll be going up and—.
If you want your money, it would be better if you come
around to the back.

Hester
Yeah.

> Hester goes. Reverend sits there, watching her leave.

FOURTH CONFESSION: REVEREND D.
"Suffering Is an Enormous Turn-on"

Reverend D.
Suffering is an enormous turn-on.
(Rest)
She had four kids and she came to me asking me what to do.
She had a look in her eye that invites liaisons
eyes that say red spandex.
She had four children four fatherless children four fatherless
    mouths to feed
fatherless mouths fatherless mouths.
Add insult to injury was what I was thinking.
There was a certain animal magnetism between us.
And she threw herself at me

like a baseball in the Minors
fast but not deadly
I coulda stepped aside but.
God made her
and her fatherless mouths.
(Rest)
I was lying in the never ending gutter of the street of the world.
You can crawl along it forever and never crawl out
praying for God to take my life
you can take it God
you can take my life back
you can have it
before I hurt myself somebody
before I do a damage that I cannot undo
before I do a crime that I can never pay for
in the never ending blistering heat
of the never ending gutter of the world
my skin hot against the pavement
but lying there I knew
that I had never hurt anybody in my life.
(Rest)
(Rest)
She was one of the multitude. She did not stand out.
(Rest)
The intercourse was not memorable.
And when she told me of her *predicament*
I gave her enough money to take care of it.
(Rest)
In all my days in the gutter I never hurt anyone.
I never held hate for anyone.
And now the hate I have for her
and her hunger
and the *hate* I have for her hunger.
God made me.
God pulled me up.
Now God, through her, wants to drag me down
and sit me at the table
at the head of the table of her fatherless house.

SCENE 7
My Song in the Street

> Hester with the kids. They are all playing freeze tag.
> After a bit, Hester is "it." She runs then stops,
> standing stock-still, looking up into the sky.
> Bully gets tagged.

Bully
1 Mississippi, 2 Mississippi, 3 Mississippi, 4 Mississippi,
5 Mississippi.

> Jabber gets tagged.

Jabber
1 Mississippi, 2 Mississippi, 3 Mississippi, 4 Mississippi,
5 Mississippi. Yr it.

> Hester gets tagged.

Hester
Hester

Jabber
Mommie?

Hester
What.

Bully
Whasswrong?

Hester
You think I like you bothering me all day?

Hester
Jabber/Bully/Trouble/Beauty

(Rest)

Hester
All yall. Leave Mommie be. She cant play right now. Shes
tired.

> Hester stands there looking up into the sky.
> The kids play apart.

Bully
Lemmie see it.

Trouble
What?

Bully
Yr pee.

Trouble
Bully

Bully
Dont got no hair or nothing on it yet. I got hair on mines.
Look.

TROUBLE
BULLY

Trouble
Jabber. Lets see yrs.

Trouble
Jabber
Bully

Bully
Its got hair. Not as much as mines though.

Beauty
I had hairs but they fell out.

Trouble
Like a bald man or something?

Beauty
Yeah.

Trouble
Trouble

Bully
Dont be touching yrself like that, Trouble, dont be nasty.

Trouble
Trouble

Jabber
You keep playing with it ssgonna fall off. Yr pee be laying in the street like a dead worm.

Trouble
Mommieeee!

Hester
Dont talk to Mommie just now.

Bully
Shes having a nervous breakdown.

Hester
Shut the fuck up, please.

(Rest)
(Rest)

Jabber
When I grow up I aint never gonna use mines.

Trouble

Not me. I be *using* mines.

Jabber

Im gonna keep mines in my pants.

Bully

How you ever gonna get married?

Jabber

Im gonna get married but Im gonna keep it in my pants.

Bully

When you get married you gonna have to get on top uh yr wife.

Jabber

I'll get on top of her all right but I'll keep it in my pants.

Trouble

Jabber, you uh tragedy.

Bully

When I get married my husbands gonna get on top of me and—

Hester

No ones getting on top of you, Bully.

Bully

He'll put the ring on my finger and I'll have me uh white dress and he'll get on top of me—

Hester

No ones getting on top of you, Bully, no ones getting on top of you, so shut yr mouth about it.

Trouble

How she gonna have babies if no one gets on top of her?

Hester

Dont *make* me hurt you!

> Hester raises her hand to Trouble who runs off.
> Bully starts crying.

Hester
Shut the fuck up or I'll give you something to cry about!

> The kids huddle together in a knot.

Hester
Jabber/Bully/Beauty
Hester
Jabber/Bully/Beauty
Hester

(Rest)

Hester
Bedtime.

Beauty
Its too early for bed—

Hester
BEDTIME!

> They hurry off.
> Hester goes back to contemplating the sky.

Hester
Hester
Hester

Hester
Big dark thing. Gods hand. Coming down on me. Blocking
the light out. 5-fingered hand of fate. Coming down on me.

> The Doctor comes on wearing his "SPAY" sandwich board.
> He watches her looking up. After a bit he looks up too.

Doctor
We've scheduled you in for the day after tomorrow. First
thing in the morning. You can send yr kids off to school

then come on in. We'll have childcare for the baby. We'll give you good meals during yr recovery. Yll go to sleep. Yll go to sleep and when you wake up, whisk! Yll be all clean. No worries no troubles no trials no tribulations no more mistakes. Clean as a whistle. You wont feel a thing. Day after tomorrow. First thing in the morning. Free of charge. Itll be our pleasure. And yours. All for the best. In the long run, Hester. Congratulations.

> The Doctor walks off. Hester is still looking up.
> Chilli walks in with his picnic basket on his arm.
> He pauses to check his pocket watch.
> Hester lowers her head.
> The sight of him knocks the wind out of her.

Hester
Oh.

Chilli
Ive been looking for you.

Hester
Oh.

Chilli
Ssbeen a long time.

Hester
I—I—.

Chilli
No need to speak.

Hester
I—

Chilli
Yr glad to see me.

Hester
Yeah.

Chilli

I been looking for you. Like I said. Lifes been good to me. Hows life been to you?

Hester

Ok. —. Hard.

Chilli
Hester

Hester

I was with the Welfare and I seed you. I called out yr name.

Chilli

I didnt hear you. Darn.

Hester

Yeah.
(Rest)
I woulda run after you but—

Chilli

But you were weak in the knees. And you couldnt move a muscle.

Hester

Running after you woulda gived you away. And Welfares been after me to know the names of my mens.

Chilli

Mens? More than one?

Hester

I seed you and I called out yr name but I didnt run after you.
(Rest)
You look good. I mean you always looked good but now you look better.
(Rest)
I didnt run after you. I didnt give you away.

Chilli

Thats my girl.

(Rest)

Welfare has my name on file, though, doesnt she?

Hester

From years ago. I—

Chilli

Not to worry couldnt be helped. I changed my name. Theyll never find me. Theres no trace of the old me left anywhere.

Hester

Cept Jabber.

Chilli

Who?

Hester

Yr son.

Hester
Chilli

Chilli

Guess what time it is?

Hester

He takes after you.

Chilli

Go on guess. Betcha cant guess. Go on.

Hester

Noon?

Chilli

Lets see. I love doing this. I love guessing the time and then pulling out my watch and seeing how close I am or how far off. I love it. I spend all day doing it. Doctor says its a tick. A sure sign of some disorder. But I cant help it. And it doesnt hurt anyone. You guessed?

Hester

Noon.

Chilli

Lets see. Ah! 3.

Hester

Oh.

> Hester goes back to contemplating the sky.

Chilli

Sorry.
(Rest)
Whats up there?

Hester

Nothing.

Chilli

I want you to look at me. I want you to take me in. Ive been searching for you for weeks now and now Ive found you. I wasnt much when you knew me. When we knew each other I was—I was a shit.
(Rest)
I was a shit, wasnt I?

Hester
Chilli

Chilli

I was a shit, agree with me.

Hester

We was young.

Chilli

We was young. We had a romance. We had a love affair. We was young. We was in love. I was infatuated with narcotics. I got you knocked up then I split.

Hester
Jabber, hes yr spitting image. Only hes a little slow, but—

Chilli
Who?

Hester
Jabber. Yr son.

Chilli
Dont bring him into it just yet. I need time. Time to get to know you again. We need time alone together. Guess.

Hester
3:02.

Chilli
Ah! 3:05. But better, yr getting better. Things move so fast these days. Ive seen the world Ive made some money Ive made a new name for myself and I have a loveless life. I dont have love in my life. Do you know what thats like? To be alone? Without love?

Hester
I got my childr—I got Jabber. hes my treasure.

Hester
Chilli

(Rest)

Chilli
Im looking for a wife.

Hester
Oh.

Chilli
I want you to try this on.

> Chilli takes a wedding dress out of his basket.
> He puts it on her, right over her old clothes.
> Hester rearranges the club, still held in her belt,
> to get the dress on more securely.

Hester
I seed you and I called out your name, but you didnt hear me, and I wanted to run after you but I was like, Hester, if Welfare finds out Chillis in town they gonna give him hell so I didnt run. I didnt move a muscle. I was mad at you. Years ago. Then I seed you and I was afraid I'd never see you again and now here you are.

Chilli
What do you think?

Hester
Its so clean.

Chilli
It suits you.

> Hester gets her shoes.

Hester
I got some special shoes. Theyd go good with this. Jabber, come meet yr daddy!

Chilli
Not yet, kid!
(Rest)
Lets not bring him into this just yet, K?

> He fiddles with his watch.

Chilli
14 years ago. Back in the old neighborhood. You and me and the moon and the stars. What was our song?

Hester
Chilli

Hester
Huh?

Chilli
What was our song?
(Rest)
Da dee dah, dah dah dee dee?

Hester
Its been a long time.

Chilli
Listen.

> Chilli plays their song, "The Looking Song,"
> on a tinny tape recorder. He sings along as she
> stands there. After a bit he dances and gets her
> to dance with him. They sing as they dance and
> do a few moves from the old days.

Chilli
Im looking for someone
to lose my looks with
looking for someone
to lose my shape with
looking for someone
to-get-my-hip-replaced with
looking for someone
Could it be you?

Im looking for someone
to lose my teeth with
looking for somcone
to go stone deef with
looking for someone
to-lie-6-feet-underneath with
looking for someone
Could it be you?

They say, "Seek and ye shall find"
so I will look until Im blind

through this big old universe
for rich or poor better or worse
Singing:
yuck up my tragedy
oh darling, marry me
let's walk on down the aisle, walk on
Down Down Down.

Cause Im looking for someone
to lose my looks with
looking for someone
to lose my teeth with
looking for someone
I'll-lie-6-feet-underneath with
looking for someone
Could it be you?

> Theyre breathless from dancing.

Chilli
This is real. The feelings I have for you, the feelings you are
feeling for me, these are all real. Ive been fighting my feelings for years. With every dollar I made. Every hour I spent.
I spent it fighting. Fighting my feelings. Maybe you did the
same thing. Maybe you remembered me against yr will,
maybe you carried a torch for me against yr better judgment.

Hester
You were my first.

Chilli
Likewise.

(Rest)

> He silently guesses the time
> and checks his guess against his watch.
> Is he right or wrong?

Chilli
"Yuck up my tragedy."

Hester
Huh?

Chilli
"Marry me."

Hester
Chilli

Hester
K.

Chilli
There are some conditions some things we have to agree on.
They dont have anything to do with money. I understand
your situation.

Hester
And my—

Chilli
And your child—ok. *Our* child—ok. These things have to
do with you and me. You would be mine and I would be yrs
and all that. But I would still retain my rights to my man-
hood. You understand.

Hester
Sure. My—

Chilli
Yr kid. We'll get to him. I would rule the roost. I would call
the shots. The whole roost and every single shot. Ive proven
myself as a success. Youve not done that. It only makes
sense that I would bc in charge.

Hester
—K.
(Rest)
I love you.

Chilli
Would you like me to get down on my knees?

Chilli gets down on his knees, offering her a ring.

Chilli
Heres an engagement ring. Its rather expensive. With an
adjustable band. If I didnt find you I would have had to,
well—. Try it on, try it on.

Chilli checks his watch. As Hester fiddles with the ring,
Bully and Trouble rush in. Beauty and Baby follow them.

Bully
Mommie!

Hester
No.

Trouble
You look fine!

Hester
No.

Beauty
Is that a diamond?

Hester
No!

Baby
Mommie!

Hester recoils from her kids.

Hester
Bully/Trouble/Beauty/Baby

Bully
Mommie?

Chilli
Who do we have here, honey?

Hester
Bully/Trouble/Beauty/Baby

Chilli
Who do we have here?

Hester
The neighbors kids.

> Chilli goes to look at his watch, doesnt.

Chilli
Honey?

Hester
Bully, wheres Jabber at?

Chilli
Honey?

Hester
Bully, Im asking you a question.

Chilli
Honey?

Trouble
hes out with Miga.

Chilli
So you all are the neighbors kids, huh?

Trouble
Who the fuck are you?

Hester
Trouble—

Chilli
Who the fuck are you?

Bully
We the neighbors kids.

Chilli
Hester

(Rest)

Chilli
Honey?

Hester
Huh?

Chilli
Im—. I'm thinking this through. I'm thinking this all the
way through. And I think—I think—.
(Rest)
(Rest)
I carried around this picture of you. Sad and lonely with our
child on yr hip. Stuggling to make do. Stuggling against all
odds. And triumphant. Triumphant against everything.
Like—hell, like Jesus and Mary. And if they could do it so
could my Hester. My dear Hester. Or so I thought.
(Rest)
But I dont think so.

> Chilli takes her ring and her veil.
> He takes her dress. He packs up his basket.

(Rest)

Hester
Please.

Chilli
Im sorry.

> Chilli looks at his watch, flipping it open
> and then snapping it shut. He leaves.

FIFTH CONFESSION: CHILLI
"We Was Young"

Chilli

We was young
and we didnt think
we didnt think that nothing we could do would hurt us
nothing we did would come back to haunt us
we was young and we knew all about gravity but gravity was a
    law that did not apply to those persons under the age of 18
gravity was something that came later
and we was young and we could
float
weightless
I was her first
and zoom to the moon if we wanted and couldnt nothing
    stop us
we would go
fast
and we were gonna live forever
and any mistakes we would shake off
we were Death Defying
we were Hot Lunatics
careless as all get out
and she needed to keep it and I needed to leave town.
People get old that way.
(Rest)
We didnt have a car and everything was pitched toward love
    in a car
and there was this car lot down from where we worked and
we were fearless
late nights go sneak in those rusted Buicks that hadnt moved
    in years
I would sit at the wheel and pretend to drive
and she would say she felt the wind in her face
surfing her hand out the window
then we'd park
without even moving
in the full light of the lot

making love—
She was my first.
We was young.
Times change.

SCENE 8
The Hand of Fate

Night. The back entrance to the Reverends new church.
Hester comes in with the kids in tow.

Hester

Sunday night. He had people in there listening to him this
morning. He passed the plate in my name. Not in my name
directly. Keeps me secret, cause, well, he has his image. I
understand that. Dont want to step on everything hes made
for himself. And he still wants me. I can tell. A woman can
tell when a man eyes her and he eyed me all right.
(Rest)
Yr building this just from talking. Must be saying the right
things. Nobodyd ever give me nothing like this for running
my mouth. Gonna get me something now. Get something or
do something. Fuck you up fuck you up! Hold on, girl, it
wont come to that.
(Rest)
[I'll only ask for 5 dollars. 5 dollars a week. That way he
cant say no. And hes got a church, so he got 5 dollars. I'll
say I need to buy something for the kids. No. I'll say I need
to—get my hair done. There is this style, curls piled up on
the head, I'll say. Takes hours to do. I need to fix myself up,
I'll say. Need to get my looks back. Need to get my teeth
done. Caps, bridges, what they called, fillers, whatever. New
teeth, dentures. Dentures. He dont cough up I'll go straight
to Welfare. Maybe.]

(Rest)

Jabber comes running around the building.
He sees Hester and sneaks up on her, touching her arm.

Jabber
Yr it.

Hester
I aint playing.

Jabber
K.

Hester
Where you been.

Jabber
Out with Miga.

Hester
Oh.

(Rest)

Jabber
Mommie?

Hester
What.

Jabber
Hester

(Rest)

Jabber
I dont like the moon.

Hester
I'll cover it up for you.

Hester holds her hand up to the sky,
hiding the moon from view.

Jabber
Whered it go?

Hester
Its gone to bed. You too.

> Hester nudges him away from her.
> He curls up with the others.

Hester
Hester

> Reverend D. comes outside.
> He carries a large neon cross.

Hester
Its Sunday.

> He sees the children.

Reverend D.
Oh God.

Hester
Its Sunday. —. Yesterday was—Saturday.

Reverend D.
Excuse me a minute?

> He props the cross against a wall.

Hester
Its Sunday.

Reverend D.
I passed the plate and it came back empty.

Hester
Oh.

Reverend D.
But not to worry: I'll have some. Tomorrow morning—

Hester
I was gonna—get myself fixed up.

Reverend D.
—When the bank opens. 100 bucks. Tomorrow morning.
All for you. You have my word.

Hester
I was thinking, you know, in my head, that there was something I can do to stop that hand coming down. Must be something—

Reverend D.
I'll have my lawyer deliver the money. Its better if you dont come back. Its too dangerous. My following are an angry bunch. They dont like the likes of you.

Hester
But you do. You like me.

Reverend D.
Youd better go.

Hester
Why you dont like me? Why you dont like me no more?

        He tries to go back inside. Hester grabs ahold of him.

Hester
Dont go.

Reverend D.
Take yr hands off me.

Hester
Why you dont like me?

              They struggle as he tries to shake her loose.
    Then, in a swift motion, Hester raises her club to strike him.
      He is much stronger than she. He brutally twists her hand.
             She recoils in pain and falls to the ground.
                   Jabber, wide awake, watches.

Reverend D.
Slut.
(Rest)
Dont ever come back here again! Ever! Yll never get nothing from me! Common Slut. Tell on me! Go on! Tell the world! I'll crush you underfoot.

He goes inside.

Hester
Hester
Hester

Jabber
Mommie.

Hester
Hester

Jabber
The moon came out again.

Jabber
Hester
Jabber

(Rest)

Jabber
Them bad boys had writing. On our house. Remember the writing they had on our house and you told me to read it and I didnt wanna I said I couldnt but that wasnt really true I could I can read but I didnt wanna.

Hester
Hush up now.

Jabber
I was reading it but I was only reading it in my head I wasnt reading it with my mouth I was reading it with my mouth but not with my tongue I was reading it only with my lips and I could hear the word outloud but only outloud in my head.

Hester
Shhhh.

Jabber
I didnt wanna say the word outloud in your head.

Hester
Hester

Jabber
I didnt wanna say you the word. You wanna know why I didnt wanna say you the word? You wanna know why? Mommie?

Hester
Hester

(Rest)

Hester
What.

Jabber
It was a bad word.

Hester
Hester

Jabber
Wanna know what it said? Wanna know what the word said?

Hester
What.

Jabber
Jabber

Hester
What?

Jabber
"Slut."

Hester
Go to sleep, Jabber.

Jabber
It read "Slut." "Slut."

Hester
Hush up.

Jabber
Whassa "Slut"?

Hester
Go sleep.

Jabber
You said if I read it youd say what it means. Slut. Whassit mean?

Hester
I said I dont wanna hear that word. How slow are you? Slomo.

Jabber
Slut.

Hester
You need to close yr mouth, Jabber.

Jabber
I know what it means. Slut.

Hester
(Shut up.)

Jabber
Slut.

Hester
(I said shut up, now.)

Jabber
I know what it means.

Hester
(And I said shut up! Shut up.)

(Rest)
(Rest)

Jabber
Slut. Sorry.

> The word just popped out, a childs joke.
> He covers his mouth, sheepishly. They look at each other.

Hester
Jabber
Hester
Jabber

> Hester quickly raises her club and hits him once.
> Brutally. He cries out and falls down dead. His cry wakes Bully,
> Trouble and Beauty. They look on. Hester beats Jabbers body
> again and again and again. Trouble and Bully back away.
> Beauty stands there watching.
> Jabber is dead and bloody.
> Hester looks up from her deed to see Beauty who runs off.
> Hester stands there alone—wet with her sons blood.
> Grief-stricken, she cradles his body. Her hands wet with
> blood, she writes an "A" on the ground.

Hester
Looks good, Jabber, dont it? Dont it, huh?

SIXTH CONFESSION: HESTER, LA NEGRITA
"I Shoulda Had a Hundred-Thousand"

Hester, La Negrita
Never shoulda had him.
Never shoulda had none of em.
Never was nothing but a pain to me:
5 Mistakes!

No, dont say that.
—nnnnnnnn—
Kids? Where you gone?
Never shoulda haddem.
Me walking around big as a house
Knocked up and Showing
and always by myself.
Men come near me oh yeah but then
love never sticks longer than a quick minute
wanna see something last forever watch water boil, you know.
I never shoulda haddem!
(Rest)

> She places her hand in the pool of Jabbers blood.

No:
I shoulda had a hundred
a hundred
I shoulda had a hundred-thousand
A hundred-thousand a whole *army* full I shoulda!
I shoulda.
One right after the other! Spitting em out with no years in
    between!
One after another:
Tail to head:
Spitting em out:
Bad mannered Bad mouthed Bad Bad *Bastards!*
A whole *army full* I shoulda!
I shoulda
—nnnnnnn—
I shoulda

> Hester sits there, crumpled, alone.
> The prison bars come down.

SCENE 9
The Prison Door

> All circle around Hester as they speak.

All
LOOK AT HER!
WHO DOES SHE THINK
SHE IS
THE ANIMAL
NO SKILLS
CEPT ONE
CANT READ CANT WRITE
SHE MARRIED?
WHAT DO YOU THINK?
SHE OUGHTA BE MARRIED
SHE AINT MARRIED
THATS WHY THINGS ARE BAD LIKE THEY ARE
CAUSE OF
GIRLS LIKE THAT
THAT EVER HAPPEN TO ME YOU WOULDNT SEE ME
    DOING THAT
YOU WOULDNT SEE THAT HAPPENING TO ME
WHO THE HELL SHE THINK SHE IS
AND NOW SHES GOT TO PAY FOR IT
HAH!

> They spit.

All
SHE DONT GOT NO SKILLS
CEPT ONE

CANT READ CANT WRITE
SHE MARRIED?
WHAT DO YOU THINK?
JUST PLAIN STUPID IF YOU ASK ME AINT NO SMART
WOMAN GOT ALL THEM BASTARDS
AND NOT A PENNY TO HER NAME
SOMETHINGS GOTTA BE DONE
CAUSE I'LL BE DAMNED IF SHE GONNA LIVE OFF ME.

All
Hester
All

Welfare
Is she in any pain?

Doctor
She shouldnt be. She wont be having anymore children.

Welfare
No more mistakes.

Chilli
Whats that?

Welfare
An "A."

Amiga Gringa
An "A."

Doctor
First letter of the alphabet.

Welfare
Thats as far as she got.

> Hester holds up her hands—theyre covered with blood.
> She looks up with outstretched arms.

Hester

Big hand coming down on me. Big hand coming down on me.
Big hand coming down on me

End of Play

The Looking Song

Words and Music by Suzan-Lori Parks

FUCKING A

An otherworldly tale involving a noble
Mother, her wayward Son, and others.
Their troubled beginning, their difficult end.
19 scenes with songs.

~ Mother Courage, Brecht.

Production History

Fucking A was originally produced by DiverseWorks (Loris Bradley, Managing/Performing Arts Director) for Infernal Bridegroom Productions (Jason Nodler, Artistic Director) on February 24, 2000, in Houston, TX. Funding was provided through a Rockefeller MAP Grant. The production was directed by the author. Scenic design was by Kirk Markley, with costume design by Danielle Wilton, lighting design by David Gipson and sound design by Douglas Robertson. Original lyrics and music were by Suzan-Lori Parks, musical direction and arrangement assistance were provided by Anthony Barilla and the music was transcribed by Randall Eng. The cast was as follows:

Hester Smith	Tamarie Cooper
Canary Mary	Amy Bruce
The Mayor	Charlie Scott
The First Lady	Amy Dickson
Butcher	Andy Nelson
Monster	Troy Schulze
Freedom Fund Lady	Lisa Marie Singerman
Scribe	Cary Winscott
First Hunter	Keith Reynolds
Second Hunter	Alexander Marchand
Third Hunter	Lisa Marie Singerman
Jailbait	Daniel Treadway
Guard	Cary Winscott
Waiting Woman #1	Lisa Marie Singerman
Waiting Woman #2	Daniel Treadway
Freshly Freed Prisoners	Daniel Treadway, Charlie Scott, Cary Winscott
Translator	Cary Winscott

Characters

Hester Smith, the Abortionist
Canary Mary, a friend of Hesters and a kept woman
The Mayor
The First Lady, his wife
Butcher
Monster
Freedom Fund Lady
Scribe
First Hunter
Second Hunter
Third Hunter
Jailbait
Guard
Waiting Woman #1
Waiting Woman #2
3 Freshly Freed Prisoners

Author's Note

The play calls for 11 actors with some doubling. The setting should be spare to reflect the poverty of the world of the play.

The play employs the foreign language of TALK. Translation for TALK may be found on page 223. The production should present a nonaudible simultaneous English translation.

PART ONE

SCENE 1

Hesters front room. Sparely furnished.
A table, two chairs and a wash bucket. This room functions
as the main room of her home. There are two doors.
One leads out the front. The other leads through
her "workroom," and out the back.
In a ceremonial altar-like place, two candles are burning.
Hester walks into the room from the workroom,
taking off her blood-spattered apron and
hanging it on a hook, lighting another candle at the altar,
then sitting at her wash bucket, wearily washing
her tools clean. She wears a simple dress
with an oddly cut-out square just above her left breast.
There we can see the large "A" deeply branded
into her skin. Bells announce the hour: midnight.

Hester
Midnight. Everyone should be in bed. But theyre not. Itd be
nice if they was all in bed and not on their way to me. Cept
the more they stay in bed the more they get in trouble. Then
they gotta come to Hester for *die Abah-nazip*. 3 babys killed
between the hours of 10 and midnight and at least one more
before the nights out if I know whats what. Their troubles yr
livlihood, Hester. Hhh. There aint no winning.

A woman stands in her front doorway.
Its Canary Mary dressed in a bright yellow dress.

Canary
Yr up.

Hester
Yr not. Yr the one should be in bed. Unless he dont want
you—

Canary
He wants me. More than ever. But tonight hes with his wife.

[handwritten: mayor?]

Hester
The Bitch.

Canary
He says he owes it to the nation to give it one last shot.

Hester
May she rot.

Canary
Lookie. A present. Lookie—

Hester
Howbout some tea?

Canary
Howbout some booze. I got a story yll love.

[handwritten: beaten down class]

Hester
Happy or sad?

Canary
Happy. So there we was—

Hester
I'd rather hear the sound of clinking coins. 5 coins a week
thats our deal. You got money but I always gotta beg.

Canary
He gives me clothes, rarely cash.
(Rest)

Drink with me. Come on. Things are getting worse between
the Mayor and his wife. Lets celebrate.

Hester
Cheers.

                                                    They drink.

Canary
The wifes at the end of her rope. He hates her. Her days are
numbered.

Hester
But he loves her money so her money buys her time. The
Rich Bitch.

Canary
This time its better. He says she makes his stomach churn.
Die la-sah Chung-chung? Sah Chung-chung lay schreck,
lay frokum, lay woah woah crisp woah-ya.

what lang.?

Hester
Rich Girl *seh tum woah Chung-chung crisp woah-ya,*
Rich Girl!

why
foreign
lang.?

Canary
Shes not the Rich Girl no more, shes our First Lady. You
should give her respect.

Hester
First Lady *teeh tum-ay wee Kazo oromakeum!*

Hester/Canary
Hahahahahahahahaha!

Canary
She dont got all the luck.

Hester
More luck than me.

Canary
Look—

Hester
May she rot—

Canary
Its a present.

Hester
—in the deepest pit for what she done to me and mine.

Canary
Lookie—

Hester
Not until my Boy comes home. Im not a true mother other-wise. When he comes home then maybe I'll forgive her but not before.

Canary
Look.

Hester
What.

Canary
Meat.

Hester
Fresh meat.

Canary
It was on yr doorstep.

Hester
On *my* doorstep?

Canary
Just sitting there. A present.

Hester

Its good meat.

Canary

Put it away so the flies wont get it.

Hester

It could be poison.

Canary

Put it away and tomorrow cook it up and invite me over. Go on.
(Rest)
No one would wanna kill you. We need you too much. Like
me, you perform one of those disrespectable but most necessary services.

Hester

Me in my bloody apron. You in yr yellow dress.

Canary

You like it? Its new. Im getting shoes to go with it.

Hester

It makes you look like a whore.

Canary

I am a whore.

Hester

Yr a kept woman.

Canary

Im a whore. Yr an abortionist Im a whore.

Hester

Cheers.
(Rest)
If Im lucky by the end of next year I'll have paid enough for
me and Boy to have a reunion picnic. Thatll take 500 coins.

all for survival.

Canary
One gold piece. Thats a lot.

Hester
I'll make it, yll see
(Rest)
Who knows what he looks like now. Hes alive. Freedom
Fund assures me of that. All growd up, thats for sure. And
tall. And a beard. And a deep voice. And a smile in his eye
like his dad had and—

Canary
Handsome.

Hester
If he takes after his dad hes good looking but dont you go
getting any ideas. Hes a good boy and when I finally buy his
freedom he'll be looking for a wife. He wont want the likes
of you.

Son = slave

Canary
The Mayor owns my exclusive rights so I wouldnt have no
time for a poor man even if he was handsome. Although
poor men got a beauty to them. But nope. The son of an
abortionist. I'd turn my nose up.

Hester
Whore.

Canary
Babykiller.

They sing "Working Womans Song":

Hester and Canary
Its not that we love
What we do
But we do it
We look at the day
We just gotta get through it.
We dig our ditch with no complaining

Work in hot sun, or even when its raining
And when the long day finally comes to an end
We'll say:
"Here is a woman
Who does all she can."   ~ Mother Courage

Canary
So there I was —

Hester
A letter came from Boy today. Its right here. Read it to me?

Canary
In a minute. Thisll make you smile. Its at her expense.

Hester
Go on.

Canary
There I was in his bed. I was in his bed and he was on top
of me and we was going at it, right? And we was screaming
and carrying on like we always do. At first we used to be so
quiet out of respect for her—

Hester
The Bitch—

Canary
Exactly. But now she aint given Hizzoner an heir or heiress
neither so what does he owe her, right? So we scream and
carry on when we go at it. And for some reason she walks
right into the room. And the Mayor and me is making so
much noise that neither of us hear her. And she is standing
right beside the bed and, you know I got my eyes open I
always do it with my eyes open cause I like to watch him
enjoy, and there she is standing there. Watching. And I look
at her. And Hizzoner sees me looking at something and he
turns his head, without a break in his screwing stride, right,
he turns his head and looks at her. Just stares at her and
keeps on screwing me. And they looked at each other like
that. It was some kind of standoff. Him screwing me and

staring at her and her staring at him and me looking back and forth from his face to her face. Then she bursts into tears and runs out of the room.

Hester
Serves her right.

Canary
Shes the only woman in the whole country who cant seem to get knocked up. Ordinarily I'd feel sorry for a woman in her position but—All that time she spent in *Europe*. All those *doctors* she seen. The mounds of drugs she takes. Nothing works. Every month *falltima Ovo ella greek Tragedy woah-ya.*

Hester
When she was a little Rich Girl she thought she owned the world. And anything she wanted she could buy. Sent my son away to prison with a flick of her little Rich Girl finger. She cant buy a son or a daughter now but I can buy mine. Im buying mine back.
(Rest)
Read the letter.

Canary
The Mayor says hes going to bump her off. Bump her off and keep her money.

Hester
Her just desserts.

Canary
Then he'll marry me he says.

Hester
You love him?

Canary
No. But he buys me anything I want.
(Rest)
Yll still be my best friend dont worry. I'll still come around. Even though you stink.

Hester
Only when a customer is on her way.

Canary
Then one must be coming.

Hester
Hmm. The only thing worse than a branded A is a stinking weeping one.

Canary
Im used to it.

> Hesters old wound, the large branded A
> above her left breast, weeps as a fresh wound would.

Hester
The A looks so fresh, like they branded me just yesterday.
(Rest)
I'll put on my apron. She'll be here in a minute. You better go.

> Hester readies for work.

Canary
Canary
Canary

(Rest)

Canary
You helped me out years ago. You didnt even know me.
I couldnt afford *die Abah-nazip*. You said I could pay you
back whenever.

Hester
And Im getting my fee plus the interest. Im a good business
woman.

Canary
Yr a good friend.

Hester

Dont overdo it.

Canary

Here. My debt and then some.

Canary gives her a gold coin.

Hester

A gold coin.

Canary

Enough for that picnic.

Hester

I'll see him this week! Canary!

Canary

Dont hug me too hard. Oh dry yr eyes, Im feeling stupid.

Hester

Thank you.

Canary

Customers not here yet. Howabout I read a little.

Canary gets the letter, opens it,
and reads it to Hester as the lights fade.

Canary

"Dear Mother. How are you? I am fine. I am doing my very best to be a good son but it is difficult to be good when surrounded by so much bad. I got two weeks time in the hold last month. No sunlight no food only water. I would tell you why I got the time but what I did was bad. But I did it to a bad person, so that aint so bad is it? . . ."

SCENE 2

The Mayor and the First Lady
in the middle of a conversation.

First Lady
Aaaaaaaaaaaaaaaaaaaaaaaaah! *Papameh! Falltimeh ma-Ovo!*
Aaaaaaaaaaaaaaaaaaah!

Mayor
Scream cry rant rave threaten me curse me denounce me
place blame gimmie the finger thumb yr nose tear yr hair
out tear my hair out kick the dog kick the servants have
some of the poor bumped off yell weep sob moan blubber
stomp yr feet curse the gods tell yr father but remind him
that not only do I have the army behind me but I answer to
the people. I must answer to the people. And those people
elected me to lead. And those people elected me to lead for
the rest of my life and when they elected me they expected
me to produce a son and they elected and expected that son
to lead for the rest of his life and so on and so on and so on
and so on and so on and —-

First Lady
My father will—

She can't give birth

Mayor
Your father will nothing. He finds your inability disgraceful.

First Lady
Im yr wife.

Mayor

And Im the Mayor. The people look up to me. They look up to me and they see my right hand dangling. Where I should be holding the hand of my son, or perhaps have my arm resting proudly on the young mans shoulder my right hand is only dangling. Empty. And they see it. And they begin to wonder what kind of man I am. I promised them a greatness that would last a hundred-thousand years but my right hand is dangling empty, Woman.

First Lady

Ive tried. I went to *Europe.* Saw all those doctors. All of them poking at me. All of them overcharging me because they all knew I was foreign. All the pills they gave me. Suitcases full. And I take them. I take them every day. Ive tried.

Mayor

Yr trying is trying the patience of the people. I cant make any more excuses for you.

First Lady

But you could spend more time with me. *Meh Kazo-say greengrass ee-sunny skies ee—*

Mayor

And ineffective.

(Rest)

Ive been thoroughly examined. Theres no question as to my effectiveness. I must say I was proud when, after an initially embarrassing moment, the mock-sexual experience into the paper cup (dont kid yrself I didnt think of you while I was at it). How embarrassing it all was. But then to see, under the microscope, all those little men swimming. An army! My own little private army!

The Mayor sings "My Little Army":

Mayor

Loyalty is the most important thing in an army
And my men have loyalty to me.

They will lay down their lives
So our state will survive.
I find that kind of courage very charming.
I salute the men of my
Little army.

Mayor
The people see your inability as a kind of treason.

First Lady
We're not at war.

Mayor
But we could be. One day.

First Lady
We are a small town in a small country in the middle of
nowhere. Small towns in small countries dont go to war.

Mayor
That kind of thinking is the kind of thinking that keeps us
back. Born with a silver spoon in yr mouth never had to
work so its no wonder you dont produce.
(Rest)
Yr a disgrace to the nation. Everyone agrees. I should
remove you from our townhouse and put you in our country
house.

First Lady
Send me to the country house and when everyones forgotten
me, yll have one of yr flunkies slit my throat.

Mayor
The people think a rest in the country may help you. Yll
have a few days to pack yr things. My hands are tied. Im
sorry. Wheres my basket?

First Lady
Right there.
(Rest)
Where are you going?

Mayor
My weekly errands. The Mayor rubs shoulders with the people. After all these years they still like it.

First Lady
One more shot. Please. Just one more.

Mayor
I have errands.

First Lady
Please.
(Rest)
Think of the nation.

First Lady
Mayor

Mayor
Fine.

First Lady
Mayor

Mayor
Come on, lets get going.

> She begins to kiss and seduce him.
> She is more passionate than he.

SCENE 3

Hester at the Freedom Fund. She states her
case to the Freedom Fund Lady.

Freedom Fund
His files here somewhere. Not to worry. We never lose anything. Of course you could just make a payment get a
receipt and I could enter it all into his file at a later time.

Hester
I dont mind waiting. Todays special. Im paying extra.

Freedom Fund
Paying extra! Wonderful. "Freedom Aint Free!" Glad you
understand our motto, Mrs. Smith.
(Rest)
Now lets see. Last name Smith first name Boy. BoySmith
BoySmith BoySmith. Its in here somewhere.
(Rest)
Look at yr A.
(Rest)
Yr an Abortionist.

Hester
Obviously.

Freedom Fund
Whats it like?

Hester
Hard.

Freedom Fund

"Someones gotta empty the toilet!" so they say. Mrs. Smith,
Abortionist. Working hard at what you do. Yr distressing
occupation. Ive never had a need of yr services, but I did
have a friend once who came to you. The public clinic had a
looong wait list—yr quick and you do the job for half the
price. Said you were very thorough. And that yr the most
discreet woman in the country. Thats something.
(Rest)
You know there are lots of women coming through this place
in need of *die Abah-nazip.* They got a man in jail or a dead-
beat lover or no money for another kid. Some women, Mrs.
Smith, lemmie tell you, *tee-tee kop fuh Binah Zoo.*

Hester
Hee la Mau Chungwoah nice-like.

Freedom Fund
Hi! Hi! Hi-Chungwoah! Teeh Kazohi-woah-ya tutti may Baza.

Hester
Woah-ya dahteh.

Freedom Fund
But what can you do? And them cleaning up their act would
put you out of yr cleaning business.
(Rest)
What did you do before you started—doing what yr doing
now?

Hester
Scrubbed floors for the Rich Family but then Boy stole from
them and they came down extra extra hard on me. It was
either prison or—

Freedom Fund
And a mother cant buy her sons freedom in prison. You chose
employment, Mrs. Smith. Youve got initiative. Thats good.

Hester
Thank you.

Freedom Fund

Well. Boy Smith. Here he is! Youve been making steady payments. Thats admirable. A prisoner can sense when his family is making steady payments. It gives them hope. How much ya paying today?

all about $.

Hester

A gold coin.

Freedom Fund

A gold coin! Hand it here! Gold!

Hester

I look forward to picnicing with my Boy this week.

Freedom Fund

Not so fast! Not so fast!
(Rest)
First lets log this in the book and put it in the bank. Gold. And of course log it in his file. Now lets see where it puts you! Yr a hard-working mother Mrs. Smith.

Hester

I am.

Freedom Fund

Oh dear.
(Rest)
Hes committed a few crimes since yr last payment.

Hester

Must be a mistake. Hes a very good boy

Freedom Fund

Of course he is. Its just that. Well, yr good boys been doing some very bad things lately.

Hester

When we have our picnic I'll tell him—

Freedom Fund
Picnic. Picnic. Picnic. Yr son wont be up for a picnic any time soon. His picnic price has doubled.

Hester
Doubled?

Freedom Fund
Im sorry.

Hester
If only that Rich Little Bitch hadnt told on him! We worked for them. They treated us worse than animals. He was only hungry! He stole some meat and she seen him and he seen her seeing him and begged her not to tell, one child to another, but she told. Went and snitched on my Boy and they took him away.
(Rest)
His price couldnt of doubled, maam.

Freedom Fund
Im sorry.

Hester
Its all that Rich Girls fault.

Freedom Fund
You cant blame her for his current incarceration. His initial three year sentence has doubled and trippled and quadrupled and—since hes been in jail hes committed several crimes.

Hester
He tells me everything. Those crimes are frame-ups every one of them.

Freedom Fund
Hes a hardened criminal, Mrs. Smith.

Hester
My sons an angel.

Freedom Fund
Angels fall.

Hester
No.
(Rest)
Ive just miscalculated his picnic price is all. Silly me.
(Rest)
Hes a good boy, maam. A very good boy.

Hester leaves.

SCENE 4

A park bench in the middle of nowhere
overlooking the sea. Monster just sits there.
After a moment Canary Mary comes by.
They sit and watch the sea.
Monster looks her over surreptitiously.

Monster
Nice view.

Monster
Canary

Monster
Nice dress.

Monster
Canary

Monster
Come here often?

Canary
Monster
Canary
Monster

Canary
You dont look familiar.

Monster
Im not. Im new. New in town.

Canary
Towns that way. About a mile.

Monster
Im in no hurry to see it. Its nice here. The sea. The air.
The sun.

Canary
The quiet.

Monster
Right.

Canary
Monster
Canary
Monster

Monster
Whatcha reading?

Canary
Words.
(Rest)
Wow. Yr arm. Thats some birthmark.

Monster
Its a scar. From a long time ago.

Canary
Does it hurt?

Monster
It did. Not no more.
(Rest)
I was in prison.

Canary
Prison?

Monster
Years ago. Someone cut me. It hurt at first. Not no more.

Monster
Canary

Monster
I heard this was a good place to meet women. They told the truth cause here you are.
(Rest)
Can I kiss you?

Canary
My lovers rich. He owns exclusive rights to me.

Monster
Oh.

Canary
Yeah.
(Rest)
Yr cute. Good luck.

> She goes on her way. He watches her go.

SCENE 5

Butcher
You drunk? Scribe?

Scribe
What.

Butcher
You drunk?

Scribe
Yeah.

Butcher
You been drunk all week.

Scribe
Yeah.

Butcher
You got someone writing in yr stead?

Scribe
Nope.

Butcher
Scribe

Scribe
You know when I first learned to write?

Butcher

When you were 3 years old.

Scribe

Howd you know that?

Butcher

Ive known you all yr life.

Scribe

We grew up together, you and me. Next door neighbors. In the hills.

Butcher

Lets get you home.

Scribe

Dad wanted me to make something of myself. So he stood over me with a stick. I still got the welts, well, the scars of the welts.
(Rest)
Perfectly formed letters at 3 years old. The most beautiful alphabet you ever seen. You seen it, Butcher, right? You seen it, right? I got it hanging —

Butcher

On the wall in yr shop. Lets go. You can show it to me.

Scribe

Naw.

Butcher

Theres lots of people wanting writing done and yr shops closed. Thats bad business.

Scribe

Butcher. It took me a whole week to get this drunk. Dont ruin it. Toast.

> Scribe toasts and drinks all by himself.
> 3 Hunters come in.

First Hunter
I shoulda gotten his balls! I shoulda gotten his balls! Im telling you I shoulda gotten his balls!

Second Hunter
You werent the first to eye him.

First Hunter
I didnt eye him first but I was the first to say: "There he is!"

Third Hunter
"There he is," so what!? Harry was pointing right at him. We all *knew* where he was.

First Hunter
But my saying it out loud alerted the dogs.

Second Hunter
You have a point.

Third Hunter
Harrys pointing alerted the dogs. When he pointed they all jerked their heads up in the air.

Second Hunter
But they didnt charge till Hank said: "There he is."

First Hunter
Which means I shoulda got the bastard convicts balls.

Third Hunter
You got the bastards feet. Thats second place. Feet arent so bad.

First Hunter
I guess.
(Rest)
They should let us keep the heads.

Second Hunter
Then howd we prove we'd caught anything?

Losers of (S)

First Hunter
You got a point.
(Rest)
Hey, Butcher!

Butcher
Hey, Hank. Hal. Harv.

First Hunter
Scribe?

Butcher
Loaded. — drunk

Third Hunter
All I got was a finger. Off the *left* hand. My wife thinks Im a loser.

Second Hunter
What can you do.

First Hunter
He screamed good, though didnt he?

Third Hunter
I can still hear it in my head. When Homer put the coals in his chest—

Second Hunter
"Why you doing this to me why you doing this to me?!" he was screaming. Like he didnt know us Hunters was gonna be on his trail when he escaped.

First Hunter
He was a nobody. Wish he'd been a famous convict. The prizes woulda been worth more and the pay woulda been better.

Second Hunter
One of my dogs broke its leg or something.

Third Hunter
I'll take a look at it later.

Second Hunter
I'd appreciate it.

They sing the "The Hunters Creed":

Hunters
We hunt
But we do
Not
Eat what we catch.
Thatd be a little much
Dontcha think?

First Hunter
Drinks on me.

He goes and gets a bottle.

Second Hunter
Hows business?

Butcher
Like yours. Lots of work and nothing to show. The Knife
Catalog came this morning.

Third Hunter
Bring it over.

First Hunter
Word is they had a convict escape up north two nights ago.
Someone wholl bring a good price too. "Monster" they call
him. "Monster!" Hes pure evil. Done everything bad there
is to do. Heres the paper, give it a read.

Third Hunter
Murder, necrophilia, sodomy, bestiality, pedophilia, armed
robbery, petty theft, embezzlement, diddling in public,
cannibalism—

Second Hunter
Whew.

First Hunter
Makes you sick, dont it?

Second Hunter
Yeah.

First Hunter
"Monster!"

Third Hunter
Just our luck though. He got out up north, we wont have a chance at spotting him down here.

Butcher
Look at that blade Hank.

First Hunter
Thats some blade.

Second Hunter
Maybe the convictll come down here. All them boats we got going to *Europe*. Maybe the convict wants to go to *Europe*.

Third Hunter
He wont be wanting to go to *Europe*. He'll be wanting to hide in the hills. In the northern hills.

First Hunter
"Monster!" Ha!

Second Hunter
Shit thats some blade Butcher.

Butcher
Show that to a pig and its skinll go Red Sea just at the sight of it.

Second Hunter
Wow.

Third Hunter

Flip to the back, lets see whats on sale.

First Hunter

I bet "Monster" comes down here.

Second Hunter

How much you betting?

First Hunter

How much you got?

> Second Hunter digs through his pockets
> counting his money. Hester comes in. She stands off
> to the side, a good distance from them,
> looking through the crowd for the Scribe.

Second Hunter

I got 12 coins. 12 coins says he aint coming.

Hunters
Hester
Hunters

Hester

I come in for the Scribe. He aint been at his stand all week.
Scribe?

Third Hunter

Wait for him outside. Yr stinking up the place.

Hester

Ive been waiting. Hey, Scribe, I got an important letter you
gotta write.

Second Hunter

Tough luck, Stinky.

First Hunter

Cover up yr A or something.

Hester

I cant its against the law.

Third Hunter

Pweeeeeeewwww!

Butcher

Harv, leave her be.

First Hunter

Shes a babykiller. Thats what she is.

Hester

Yr daughters been a customer of mine. More than once.

[handwritten: ouch.]

First Hunter

Shut yr trap!

Hester

*Le doe-dunk eyesee Frahla ehle dunk sehh Frahla ah ma,
Mister Hunter.*

Second Hunter

Thats private family business. I'll smash yr face for blab-
bing that!

Butcher

Hal! Hey! You got better things to do than hit a woman. *[handwritten: ✗]*

Second Hunter
Butcher

[handwritten: ~ Baker - (Mother Courage)]

First Hunter

Didnt know you spoke TALK. *[handwritten: haha.]*

Second Hunter

Just enough to get by. *[handwritten: civilized speaking]*

First Hunter

My wife wants me to learn it but I say no way. Keep that
stuff private. Like it should be. Thats what I say.

Second Hunter
Butcher

Third Hunter
10 coins says the convictll come our way. Another 3 says I'll
sight him first.

First Hunter
Drinks on me!

Butcher
Come on, Scribe. You got work to do.
(Rest)
He'll get up in a minute.

Hester
I'll wait outside.

> Hester goes outside. Butcher helps
> Scribe to his feet. The Hunters sing
> their song again:

Hunters
We hunt
But we do
Not
Eat what we catch.
Thatd be a little much
Dontcha think?

SCENE 6

Hester walks along the street with her freshly written letter.

Hester
"Darling Son," it says. "Its spring again and so Im outside
scrubbing the marble walk. Every day I wake at dawn and
scrub. The same walkway Ive scrubbed every spring since
we went to work for them. They arent as mean as when we
worked here together. Ive got plenty to eat and hope you do
too. Love, Ma." Wish I had enough coins to include more.
Well. This is good enough. Next year we'll be picnicing.
We'll have meat and cheese and wine and bread and apples.
(Rest)
No shame in telling a lie. "I still work for the Rich People."
Ha! Better to lie than to have him ashamed cause his moth-
ers a babykiller.
(Rest)
"Darling Son!" it says, "Its spring again and so Im—"

The First Lady passes by.
She tries to dodge Hester but Hester confronts her.

Hester
First Lady

Hester
Bitch.

First Lady
Excuse me.

Hester

Bitch. I hear hes sending you away! You deserve it!

The First Lady hurries on her way as
Hester shouts curses at her.

Hester

Suptah nekkie frokrisp Chung-chung! Noonka Bleehc tryohla die. Noonka! Grope tillie not. Grope say Basket shreck eey grope say winduptrala! Grope sah Tupdom linke die like um die Nassum. Grope sah Ovoweh miss eeh so quaknie! Grope sah Milch shreck eeh naymilch noonkey treben! Noonke!

After spending her anger,
Hester pauses to catch her breath
and then continues on her way.

SCENE 7

> The Mayor fully dressed. Canary in her underwear.
> Mayor takes off his clothes. Canary angrily gets dressed.
> Mayor gets dressed.

Mayor
Yr sore.

Canary
Im not sore.

Mayor
Good. Get naked.

> She takes off her clothes.
> As he gets partly undressed,
> she gets partly dressed.

Canary
Mayor

Canary
I'd like a ring. A ring aint too much to ask.

Mayor
I told her to go to the country but she wont go. She knows
whats up.

Canary
Ring Ring! Ring Ring!
(Rest)
Yr tired of me.

Mayor
I cant think of rings right now.
(Rest)
Planning a murder takes a lot of thought. Shes got to be
wiped out just right so that the blame falls on some nobody
and not at all on me or my office. Ive got to be kept in the
clear.

Canary
Have one of yr lieutenants do it. Or a sniper. I'll do it if you
want.

Mayor
You would?

Canary
One of yr lieutenants would make it more—professional.

Mayor
Yr right.

Canary
She'll be dead. Yll weep at her funeral. Yll get all her
money. Yll marry me.

Mayor
My wife will die a tragic death. I will stand like the soldier
that I am as they put her in the deep dark ground. My
chest will heave in sadness but no tears will fall. I am their
soldier-Mayor. Not a tear will fall. She will have left me all
her money. I will hang my head and the people will want me
to lift my head up. The people will demand that I remarry.
(Rest)
They will demand that I remarry a woman of a—of a certain
background. My heart will be split in two. Each night with
my new wife I will dream of you. I am their humble civil
servant. I cannot let them down.

cannot marry the whore

Canary
You will let them down by replacing one *kaltie Bleehc* with
another.

Mayor
As their Mayor Im prepared to sacrifice my pleasure.
Besides. Nothing between us will change. I'll be remarried.
And in good time I'll be a father, so I'll be more relaxed.
But nothing between us will change.

Canary
You said youd marry me.
(Rest)
You gave your word.
(Rest)
I love you.

Mayor
I have the future of my country to consider.

Canary
You are the Mayor they are the people. You are the shepherd they are the sheep. You set the clock you style the fashion you define the taste.

Mayor
They elected me—

Canary
To rule for a hundred thousand years.

Mayor
How many days is that? How many hours how many minutes.

Canary
How many kisses?
(Rest)
Marry me.
(Rest)
Im begging on my knees.

Mayor
Canary
Mayor
Canary

Mayor
Heres some gold.

Mayor
Canary

Mayor
"Wife," "Mistress," what does it matter? Take the gold. Buy
something nice.

> He gives her several gold coins.

Canary
Sweetheart.

Mayor
Good girl.

> A gentle moment then she steps away.
> She sings "Gilded Cage":

Canary
I dreamed I met a lioness
She once lived in the wild
She once hunted for all her food
She once was so self-styled
She once roamed anywhere she pleased
She once was free and brave
But in my dream she spoke to me
From a gorgeous gilded cage.

Her gilded cage was solid gold
The bars shone like sunshine
She'd gone in there all on her own
No one had forced her
This time.
"Freedom," she said, "aint free at all.
Its price: a heavy wage
And when you find how much your freedom costs
You just may give it up
For a gorgeous gilded cage."

SCENE 8

That park bench in the middle of nowhere
overlooking the sea. The First Lady sits there crying.
After a moment Monster comes by.
He looks her over surreptitiously
then sits and watches the sea.
She notices him and composes herself.

Monster
First Lady

Monster
Nice view.

Monster
First Lady

Monster
Nice dress.

Monster
First Lady

Monster
Come here often?

First Lady
Monster
First Lady
Monster

First Lady
Im sad.

Monster
Im not.
(Rest)
Im new. New in town.

Same trick.

First Lady
Im sad.

Monster
Yr beautiful.
(Rest)
Beautiful like the ocean only the ocean is moving and you
are. Still.
(Rest)
I always wanted to meet a woman like that.

First Lady
My husband doesnt want me.

Monster
Cant be true. Someone as beautiful as you.

First Lady
Monster

First Lady
Gosh. Yr arm. Thats some birthmark.

Monster
Its a scar. From a long time ago.

First Lady
Does it hurt?

Monster
It did. Not no more.
(Rest)
Thats the trick with things that hurt. Outlast them, they stop
hurting. Sooner or later.

First Lady
You think?

Monster
Thats been my experience.

First Lady
Monster
First Lady
Monster

First Lady
May I kiss you?

> She kisses him. They kiss.

SCENE 9

Hesters home. Late at night. The room is dark.
She comes in through the back door.
Shes wearing her bloody apron, having just finished
another abortion. She throws her tools into
the wash bucket and, going over to the altar-like place,
lights a candle. The candle illuminates the room
and she sees someone sitting there:
Butcher, also in his bloody apron.

Hester
Butcher. Well. Its late.

Butcher
You should lock your door. Theres another convict on the loose.

Hester
Most people think its bad luck coming here.
(Rest)
Yll have bad luck now.

Butcher
I got bad luck already.

Hester
Butcher

Hester
I must be way behind in my meat bill. I know yr a man who likes his customers to pay their bills on time.

Butcher
Hester—

Hester
Freedom comes first. I pay the Freeodom Fund on time, or
they add on extra. They miscalculated recently. It really set
me back. But ha! I came into some more money earlier
today. Another wonderful gift from a very good friend. I
guess you heard about it and are here looking for whats
owed you but Im going to the Fund again tomorrow and pay
on my sons freedom. Its not enough to spring him but this
time for sure itll get us the picnic lunch. For sure this time.
Ive checked and rechecked the figures. This time for sure
we'll be eating together by the end of the week. Me and Boy.
After 30 years. You gotta understand, my meat bills—

Butcher
Zero. You dont owe.

Hester
Oh.

(Rest)

Butcher
Canary give you the money?

Hester
Yes. Another gold coin. Just a little while ago. She really
wants to help out.

Butcher
Thats good of her.

Hester
Shes a good friend.

Hester
Butcher

Butcher
Sit. Sit with me.

> She sits. Theyre both sitting there
> in their bloody aprons.

Butcher

It was nice seeing you the other day.

Hester

Scribe wrote me a good letter. Thanks for getting him on his feet.

Hester
Butcher

Hester

He makes the nicest looking letters. Even when hes sloshed. Such pretty shapes, straight bold lines and gentle curls. Makes me wish I could read. And write too.

Butcher

You should learn.

Hester

Well.

Butcher

Its not that hard. I could teach you.
(Rest)
If you learned writing you could write yr son yrself, save money on Scribe and spend less time working.
(Rest)
And I'd be happy to teach you. Itd be my pleasure.

Hester
Butcher

Hester

You got a daughter locked up too, dontcha?

Butcher

Shes a bad seed. same shoes

Hester

Its hard to be good when surrounded by so many bad people.

Butcher

My kid, Lulu. Rotten to the core she is. Always was. From day one, that Lulu. She was always into something bad.

(Rest)

[Prostitution, racketeering, moneylaundering, cyber fraud, intellectual embezzlement, highway robbery, dialing for dollars, doing a buffalo after midnight, printing her own money, cheating at cheating, jaywalking, selling herself without a license, selling her children without a permit, unlawful reproduction, having more than one spouse, claiming to have multiple parents, claiming to have multiple orgasms, claiming to have injuries she didnt have, claiming to have been places she never was, making love at gunpoint, indecent exposure, hanging upside down in a public place, walking in the rain without a flashlight, walking home from work without a pink slip, taking up more than one seat of the public conveyance, not saluting the authorities, having no known address, skipping school, skipping her monthly, smoking in the girls room, drugging of all stripes and varieties, taking and dispensing narcotics without a permit, smiling in the off season, hunting on private land, lying on private grass, trespassing, eating from the table of authority, fornicating with the Other, overdue shit at the LendingSpot, general physical underdevelopment, looking up too much, looking into the eyes of her arresting authority, taking a crap in the office of said arresting authority, playing with herself on the governments nickel, aiding and abetting a whole host of things, admitting to participating in a boondoggle, running red lights, general dismemberment, congregating without a permit, speaking her mind without a permit, not wearing drawers, leaving her lights on, playing loud music, fighting the power, passing the buck, not paying the electric, obscene phone calls, ringing and running, conversations with children who were not her own thus implanting strange notions in the minds of minors, conversations with adults which bordered on the ridiculous, fornicating with the same sex, fornicating with young men under the age of 15 and old men over the age of her old mans age, saying she was mar-

ried when she wasnt, having no sense of direction, grand
larceny, petty theft, hotwiring, image manipulation, leading
unsuspecting men and women into cyberspace and leaving
them there lost and without a roadmap, riding without a
helmet, fraternizing with known felons, copulating with said
known felons with the intent to reproduce, espionage, high
treason, mutiny at sea, operating a dumptruck without a
license, having improper identification, slave trading, horse
stealing, murder in the first degree, not knowing what time
it is, talking too much, laughing out of turn, murder in the
second degree, standing on one leg in a 2-legged zone,
jumping the turnstile, jumping the turnstilee, burning down
the house, murder in the nth degree, failing to perform life-
saving procedures in a situation that warranted it, aiding
and abetting a forest fire, failing to predict a series of natural
disasters, perjury, not pulling her weight, not wearing her
teeth, fingering the Commander, selling state secrets, not
believing in The Afterlife, defaming the name of the State,
passing as a persona non grata, defacing animates and
intimates alike, persuading, dumping pollutants, not doing
her bit, having neither gimmick nor schtick, mugging i.e.
pulling faces, mugging i.e. sticking up—you get the gist—
having bad timing, possessing a firearm, not eating her
vegetables, being a bad apple, falling too far from the tree,
possessing a concealed freakish attribute, harboring the
convicted, fencing the stolen, giving false testimony, raising
the dead, envisioning the future, remembering the past,
speeding—huh. *trying to live.*
(Rest)
(Rest)

Hester
Impressive.]

Butcher
Shes not eligible for the Freedom Fund Program.

Hester
I wouldnt think she would be.
(Rest)
My Boys an angel who had a little bad luck.

Butcher
Thats life.

Hester
Butcher

Butcher
Butcherings the only thing I ever wanted to do. I feel like
Im right in the middle of the great chain of being. Passing
life from one group to another. Sure I kill them but I make
sure it never hurts. Ive spent all my life perfecting the painless slaughter. Lemmie show you.

> With his sheathed knife in hand he comes to her,
> standing behind her, putting the knife
> near her throat, instructing her.

Butcher
Yr slaughtering a pig. Smart animal. Also very bloody. You
put him between yr legs with his back toward you. Lift up
his head and quick! Slice quick. They cry out but its only
reflex. Ive read all the anatomy books. This kind of cut is
completely painless.
(Rest)
You try.

> They switch places. Hester gives it a try.

Hester
Like this?

Butcher
Faster and dont bear down so hard. The knife is sharp. You
dont want him feeling a thing. Like the cold wind crossed
his throat, thats all.

Hester
Like this?

Butcher
Thats it. Once more.

Hester
Ha!

Butcher
Good Job!

Hester
Thank you.

Butcher
Hester

Hester
Would you like to see
my gold coin?

Butcher
Ive brought you a present.

Hester
Butcher

Hester
Before I give it to the Fund
lemmie show you.

Butcher
Its not much. Just meat. But
its a good cut.

She holds up her coin. He shows a neatly tied package.

Hester
Pretty aint it?

Hester
Butcher

Hester
It was you who left the meat
the other day.

Butcher
Ive wanted you.
For a long time.

He gives her the package of meat.

Hester
That was real nice. The meat. It cooked up good.

Butcher
Yr lovely.

Hester

Oh, Im a regular princess, with my branded A—

Butcher

I always figured you wanted to be alone—

Hester

—that weeps and stinks.

Butcher

—but I figured I would try.

Hester

Dont make fun of me. "Yr lovely." Sure. Me and my bloody bloody apron.

Butcher

(Rest)

Theres no shame in a bloody apron.

Hester
Butcher

He takes her hand. She nervously takes it away.

Butcher

Whenever I see you yr always sitting or standing with yr left shoulder pulled back. Yr A is as plain as day but you dont want no one seeing it. You shouldnt be ashamed.

Hester

I dont like people staring.

Butcher

Why do they brand you aborters? They dont brand us butchers.

Hester

The brand comes with the job is all I know. "And the brand must be visible at all times." Thats the law. Everyone knows

what I do—but then, my A is also like a shingle and a
license, so nobody in needll ever get suckered by a charlatan.
(Rest)
What we do is bad. And good. And bad and good and good
and bad. Theres no easy way to look at it.
(Rest)
Go to prison or take this job. That was my choice. Choose A
or choose B. I chose A.

Butcher
You got a chance to get him out this way.

Hester
Thats the way I see it.

Butcher
And you provide a service. You chose right.

Hester
Thank you.

Butcher
You should put that coin in a safe place.

Hester
Good thinking.

> She looks around quickly and decides
> to put the coin in her shoe.

Butcher
You must be excited about yr reunion picnic.

Hester
And a little nervous.

Butcher
Its a wonder yll even recognize him, what with the time
thats passed and the ways hes changed.

Hester
I'll know my Boy.

Butcher
By his looks?

Hester
Better than that.
(Rest)
When they comed to take him away, just before they took
him, I bit him. Hard. Right on the arm just here. I bit hard.
Deep into his skin. His blood in my mouth. He screamed
but then he was screaming anyway. After theyd tooked him
away I went and bit myself. Just as hard and in the same
place exactly. See the mark I got? My Boys got one too.
Identical.

> She shows him her bite mark scar,
> on the inside of her left forearm,
> the remains of a horrid wound.

Butcher
Hes a grown man now.

Hester
He'll always have my mark.
(Rest)
You think my A is ugly.

Butcher
No.

Hester
But you could never love it.

Butcher
Loving anything is hard.

Hester
Butcher

> He takes her hand again.
> This time she doesnt pull away.

Hester

It would be nice. But you cant *spend the night.*
(Rest)
Too many people would see you leaving in the morning. You
may not care but I care.

Butcher

K.

> They sit there holding hands.
> The backdoor bell rings.

Butcher

Yr bell.

Hester

(Rest)
Let it ring.

> The bell rings again, this time more insistently.
> Hester makes no move to get up and answer it.

SCENE 10

Hesters house. The next morning. Dawns early light.
Monster rummaging around Hesters front room
looking for things to steal. He finds the meat,
smells it and gobbles at it.
Offstage Hester begins singing.
She sings a version of "Working Womans Song"
to herself as she enters the room.
Monster hears her and hides himself.

Hester
I love what we do when we do it we do it
I fall in his arms and he puts me through it.
I take his love with no complaining
He takes my love, even when its raining . . .

Monster grabs her.

Monster
Gimmie all yr money and all yr food or I'll kill you.

Hester
I dont got much.

Monster
Yve got hiding places. Ha! A gun!

He spies a rusty shotgun above the mantel.
Takes it down.

Monster
Its old. Does it work?

Hester
Sometimes. Its very rusty.

Monster
Forget it.

                                    He tosses the gun down.

Monster
Wheres yr money at?

Hester
Monster

Monster
Dont give it up and I'll kill you.

            Hester goes to a drawer, pulls it out, reaches behind it,
                    withdraws money, hands it to him.
            As he takes the money from her he sees her scar.
                He takes a good long look, then plays it off.

Hester
Monster

Hester
Thats all.

Monster
Monster

Hester
Thats all. On my life thats all.

Monster
Monster

Hester
Yr staring at me.

Monster
No Im not.

Hester
I gave you all my money.

Monster
Good.
(Rest)
I said I woulda killed you and I woulda. Just so you know.

Hester
Monster

> Monster hurries out the front door.
> Hester stands as if rooted to the spot.
> Then, breathing a sigh of relief, she hurries to the
> window to make sure he is on his way.
> She then takes off her shoe and takes out the gold coin,
> holding it triumphantly up to the light.

butcher was right!!

SCENE 11

The Hunters come in deep in conversation.

Second Hunter
I dont mind losing the bet. Not at all dont get me wrong.

Third Hunter
Thats why he bet you.

Second Hunter
Exactly. I knew I would lose.

First Hunter
I dont get it.

Third Hunter
Reverse psychology.

Second Hunter
Exactly.

First Hunter
Reverse psychology on who, on me?

Second Hunter
On the convict.

Third Hunter
Very smart.

First Hunter

I dont get it.

Third Hunter

Hal was psyching out that convict.

First Hunter

"Monster!"

Third Hunter

We shouldnt get on a first name basis with him.

First Hunter

Why not? "Monster!" Im not scared to say his name. And we'll get real close to him soon enough—

Second Hunter

Cause I bet you. I bet you that he *wouldnt* come down.
I place such a bet knowing Im an unlucky guy, and there-
fore knowing that I would more likely than not *lose* the bet
and that me *losing* the bet would mean he was coming. Me
betting you exerted a psychic pull on him.

Third Hunter

Hals bad luck works like a charm.

First Hunter

Im giving you yr money back.

Second Hunter

Yr all right, Hank.

Third Hunter

Whens the last time we did a runthrough? You cant remember, right? Cause its been years.

First Hunter

Its been years cause its lots of work.

Third Hunter

Its also a lot of fun.

Second Hunter
Whats a runthrough?

Third Hunter
The best thing to do to a convict when you catch him. It gets the loudest screams.

First Hunter
You get a hot iron rod and run it up his bottom and out his throat.

Third Hunter
Then you stick the rod in the ground and let him wiggle on the stick.

Second Hunter
Shit.

First Hunter
You wouldnt think they would wiggle for long but they do.

Third Hunter
And the screams—

Second Hunter
Im game to try if you all are.

Third Hunter
We're gonna find him, I can feel it. And besides getting rich off the money he'll make us, we'll have some fun.

First Hunter
Say it come on say it.

Second Hunter
Monster!

Third Hunter
Monster!

Second/Third Hunters
Monster! MONSTER!

First Hunter
Come on lets get to work.

They go on their way.

Hunting of Monster

SCENE 12

picnic

> Hester waiting. She wears a shawl that conceals her A.
> She looks at the sky and notes the time. She keeps waiting.
> She opens the picnic basket, examines the contents, closes
> the basket. She primps. She waits.
> She opens the basket, takes out a checked cloth
> and spreads it on the ground. She sits down on the cloth.
> Practices "meeting" her son.

Hester

He sees me on the ground like this he may think I shrunk.
I'll stand.
(Rest)
"Son!" Too eager.
(Rest)
"Son." Not eager enough.
(Rest)
I look like Im waiting for a bus.
(Rest)
Kneeling. This is good. Kneeling in thanks. Put the past
behind us and lets be thankful for this sunny picnic
day—although he'll think Ive lost my legs. I'll stand.

> Far far away, a Guard brings Jailbait out.
> They stand together. The Guard wears a luncheon napkin
> at his chin and fills out paperwork on a clipboard.
> Jailbait wears shackles on his feet.

Guard

Just stand here. I'll take you to the picnic ground in a
minute.

Jailbait
Wheres she at?

Guard
Just behind that fence there.
(Rest)
You should be happy. Shes yr mother.

Jailbait
What about my meal?

Guard
Shes bringing you a picnic. Real food. Yr lucky. I'll come
get you in an hour or so.

Jailbait
Yr leaving me?

Guard
Its lunchtime for us too.

Jailbait
You aint scared I'll make a run for it?

Guard
Youre wearing a chain. So if you run you wont run far.
Besides, yr moms visiting. And shes brought you a picnic.

Jailbait
I dont got no mom.

Guard
Sure you do. Everybodys got a mom. Even you.

> The Guard walks Jailbait toward Hester.

Guard
Here he is, maam. Enjoy yrselves.

> The Guard goes back inside.
> She sees him and they stand still, staring at each other.

Hester

Jailbait

Hester

Jailbait

Hester

(Son.)

Jailbait

Hester

> He just looks at her, doesnt move. She walks to him.
> Hugs him gently then harder. He does not respond.
> She bursts into tears.

Hester

Waaaaahhhhhhhhhh!

Jailbait

Jailbait

> She cries for quite some time.
> He stands there, mildly interested, mostly bored.

Hester

Its you.

Jailbait

I guess.

Hester

My child my love my son its you.

> She hugs him very hard.
> With some difficulty, he struggles free.

Jailbait

They said you had food.

Hester

—Yes. I have food.

(Rest)
30 years. Well.
(Rest)

Lets see yr mark. The mark yr mother gave you all those
years ago. People thought I was crazy. "I'll know my Boy
anywhere," I said! Look at mine! See! My teeth marks! Yrs
is identical! Lets see how it healed.

Jailbait
Dont touch me. ⟶ hot her son?

Hester
Jailbait

Hester
All these years locked up in this horrible place. "Dont
touch me." Of course.
(Rest)
((Im going to get you out soon. Ive got friends with gold. But
youve got to help. You keep befriending those bad people
theyll keep blaming things on you. Make nice friends, son.
Promise me.))

Jailbait
Im hungry.

Hester
Of course yr hungry. See? A whole basket full of wonderful
things. Lets see your arm. Just a peek.

Jailbait
Hands off.

Hester
Oh.

Jailbait
Can we eat, please?
(Rest)
Mother?

Hester
Waaaaaaah!

> She cries again. He grabs the basket and
> begins eating. She collects herself.

Jailbait
I usually eat with my hands. Dya mind?

Hester
Not at all.

> He eats like an animal.

Hester
Youve grown so much.
(Rest)
Yr such a man.

Jailbait
Hester

Jailbait
Thanks.

> He goes back to eating.

Hester
Do I look old? Probably, right? But not too old I hope.
(Rest)
(Rest)
Lets see that mark I gave you. Just a quick look. I want to
know what kind of scar its made. Take another look at mine.
Kinda pretty, I think. I did them both in such a hurry but
they turned out well. What do you think? Kind of looks like
a heart. Like Im wearing my heart on my sleeve or some-
thing. Hahahahaha. Lemmie see yrs.

Jailbait
Quit grabbing at me!

Hester
Sorry.
(Rest)
Could I pet you, son?

Jailbait
Where?

Hester
On the head.

Jailbait
Go ahead.

> She pets him very lightly on the head.

Jailbait
Yr looking at me like you wanna eat me up.

Hester
Motherlove.

Jailbait
Heavy.
(Rest)
What else you bring for me?

Hester
Cake.

Jailbait
Show.

> He takes the entire cake and eats.

Hester
Look what living here has done to you. Eating yr food with
yr eyes scouring the countryside as if someones gonna rush
up and snatch yr goodies! Like this!

> She playfully snatches his food.
> He fiercely grabs it back.

Hester
Jailbait

Hester
I brought wine.

Jailbait
Break em open.

> She opens both bottles. He grabs them and
> gluts them down. Some of the wine makes it
> down his throat, some of it goes down his shirt.

Jailbait
You know whatd be great? Lemmie put my head in yr lap
and you tell me a story. Thatd be great.

Hester
Ok. Once upon a time you were little and I was young and
everything was nice.

Jailbait
And I wasnt bad?

Hester
You were never bad. They tell me yr bad but I dont believe
them. You shouldnt believe them either.
(Rest)
Lets see yr mark.

> She gingerly searches his forearm. He lets her.

Jailbait
You like looking at me dont you?

Hester
I thought I put it on the same arm I put mine on. Maybe
I put it on the other. Its been a long time.

Jailbait
You smell good. You wearing perfume?

> She goes to look at his other arm.

Hester

Im going to look at yr other arm, ok?

Jailbait

I wanna look at your other arm.

> He rolls up her sleeve, bites her arm playfully. She laughs.

Hester

Stop that! Now what are you doing?

> He is burying his face in her lap.

Hester

Yr tickling me, son. Son, what are you doing?

Jailbait

Im getting romantic. Yr picnic got me hot.

oh gosh...

Hester

Stop that, son.

Jailbait

That son crap may turn you on, lady, but it kinda breaks the mood for me, if you know what I mean.

Hester

Dont touch me like that.

Jailbait

Yr not no virgin are you?

Hester

Stop it, baby.

Jailbait

I aint no baby, Mama, Im a full grown man.

Hester
Theyd lock you up for good if they came out here and saw you getting fresh with your own mother.

Jailbait
I love you.

Hester
Boy, stop that!

Jailbait
Boy? I aint Boy. My names Joe.

Hester
Jailbait

Hester
Yr not my son.

Jailbait
Sorry. His names—

Hester
Boy. His name is Boy. Boy Smith.

Jailbait
Funny name. I could say I never heard of him but I have.
(Rest)
(Rest)
Smashed his brains in myself. Hes dead.
(Rest)
I guess thats why they sent me to you in his place.

Hester
Dead.

Jailbait
Bad things happen. All the time. But hey, no use crying.

Hester
Hester
Hester

Jailbait

You gonna gimmie some or what?

Hester
Hester
Hester

Jailbait

The way I see it we got ourselves some minutes left. And I
always had a thing for older women.

> Jailbait kisses her and feels her up.
> Hester, struck dumb with grief and disbelief,
> lets Jailbait do what he wants. He touches and
> gropes her and she sits there, flicking at his hands
> from time to time as if she were flicking at flies.
> After a moment the action stops.
> Hester sings "My Vengeance":

Hester

The low on the ladder
The barrels rock bottom
Will reach up and strangle
The Rich then God rot them.
She'll mourn the day
She crushed us underfoot.
Her Rich Girl wealth
Will not stop me from put-
ting my mark on her
And it will equal what we've paid.
My vengence will show her
How a true mother is made.

> Jailbait embraces her again and the rape continues.

being raped

PART TWO

SCENE 13

> Monster and First Lady sitting on that same park bench.
> Wanted posters of Monster hang all over the place.
>
> Monster smokes.

First Lady
I didnt know you smoked.

Monster
First Lady

Monster
You got my note.

First Lady
Im here.

Monster
I guess you got it.
(Rest)
You knocked up?

First Lady
No.

Monster
You sure?
(Rest)
If yr knocked up its mine.

(Rest)
Keep it, okay? Something to remember me by.

First Lady
Im not—expecting.

Monster
Too bad.
(Rest)
Whats yr husband do?

First Lady
Nothing.

Monster
I seen yr house. Its a big house. Right in the middle of town. He must do something.

First Lady
Hes in business.

Monster
I figured. A tycoon, right?

First Lady
Thats right. A tycoon.

Monster
I want some money.

First Lady
How much.

Monster
A lot. I wanna live in style. I dont see why I shouldnt, do you?

First Lady
How much.

Monster
5 thousand coins.

First Lady
How about 3—

Monster
How about 10. Thousand. 10 thousand.
(Rest)
Say its a deal. Come on. Agree. You cant con an ex-con.

First Lady
You were in prison.

Monster
Yeah.

First Lady
Oh.

Monster
Why you holding yr stomach. You knocked up?

First Lady
Im sick.

Monster
Sure you arent knocked up?

First Lady
Yr the one theyre all looking for. Yr the man on the loose,
arent you?

Monster
You gonna snitch? You look like yr gonna snitch.

First Lady
Yr pictures all over town.

Monster
You ever snitch?

First Lady
(Rest)
No.

Monster

Good.

(Rest)

Hear the bells? Theyre ringing noon. The next time they ring 12 itll be midnight.

(Rest)

Bring me my money. 10 thousand coins. At midnight tonight.

First Lady

I'll turn you in.

Monster

I'll kill you first. Believe it.

First Lady
Monster

Monster

12 midnight tonight. Go on. Get going. You got a lot of diamond rings to sell, Im sure. Thats it, hold yr stomach. I knocked you up, didnt I ? Didnt I?!

She hurries away.

SCENE 14

Oustide Hesters back door. Two women waiting.

Waiting Woman #1
Weh noonka Flowmeh. Weh pak Nah rum—

Waiting Woman #2
Weh nim ohnio Zamen die sah "noonka schwang," rum—

Waiting Woman #1
Weh nam laisah sah Zamen. Woah-ya priceypricey eeh Beardkum der dak Zamensah like-a-rug woah.

Waiting Woman #2
Tah humble.

Waiting Woman #1
Tah humble si.

(Rest)

Waiting Woman #2
Why dont she answer her bell?

Waiting Woman #1
Sign says "Closed." Maybe she closed for good. Maybe she quit the business.

Waiting Woman #2
I dont blame her. Mrs. Smith! Hey! Hey in there! Hey! Hey!

First Lady enters fresh from her encounter
with Monster. She is heavily veiled and
holds her stomach.

Waiting Woman #1
Look.

Waiting Woman #2
Well. A rich lady. Lah-dee-dah.

Waiting Woman #1
Dont make fun.
(Rest)
Who is she you think?

Waiting Woman #2
Who knows.
(Rest)
Ya come to Hester Smith cause she'll let you keep yr veil on
and wont ask no questions, huh?

First Lady
Im here same as you.

Waiting Woman #1
Loverboys seed growing inside you, huh?

Waiting Woman #2
You got the guilties and needs to get rid of it before the husband finds out.

First Lady
Yes.

First Lady
First Lady
First Lady

(Rest)

190   Suzan-Lori Parks

First Lady
No. Not at all.
(Rest)
One seed is as good as another. And when the husband resembles the lover, he wont be none the wiser.

Waiting Woman #1
Smart thinking.

Waiting Woman #2
Real real smart thinking.

First Lady sings "My Little Enemy":

First Lady
They say Fidelity
Is the most important thing
When yr married.
But its such a pricey luxury.
When yr up against the wall
Yll take a poke from some poor slob.
The child Im growing will be my salvation.
Who knows, he may grow up to rule the nation.
And my husband, blind with happiness,
Will never guess
The enemy in his army.

First Lady
Thank you. Here. Spend this for me.

She gives them money and goes.

Waiting Woman #1
Rich folk.

Waiting Woman #2
Yeah.

SCENE 15

> Hesters home. She sits in a big tin tub.
> Canary scrubs her back, giving her a bath.

Canary
Am I scrubbing you too hard?

Hester
Hester

Canary
Theyre reconciled again. Word is she went to her daddy
crying and he put out more money. And they spent last
night together. I lay in his bed waiting and he was with her.
Oh, what money can do.
(Rest)
Warm water sweet soap and gentle scrubbing. Does it feel
good?

Hester
I could cut her head off.

Canary
Inhale. Soap smells good, dont it?

Hester
Youd put sleeping powder into her bedtime snack. I'd sneak
into her big house, find her room, and cut her head off.

> Hesters backdoor bell rings.

Canary

Yr A is weeping. You got folks out there. 3 a minute ago but now only 2. The "Closed" signs on the door. Hester aint helping no one but herself today.

Hester

I could follow her on one of her afternoon constitutionals and jump out from behind a tree and strangle her with my bare hands.

Canary

Freedom Fund confirmed hes dead but I dont believe them and you shouldnt believe them neither. If hes dead whose been writing you all these years? Theyve just misplaced him. He'll turn up. Yll see.

Hester

Take my knife and stab her till theres nothing left of her but wounds. Then we'd be equal.   *vengeance*

Canary

The Fund says yr due for a full refund.
(Rest)
I dont believe hes dead. But you could take the money anyway. You could retire.

Hester

I could slit her throat.   *rage*

Canary

(Rest)
Do you know how many men and women they got locked up? More thans walking free in the streets thats how many. Its a wonder they aint lost them all. Prisoners get lost all the time, I'll bet. Sounds crazy but thats what kind of crazy world we live in. Something crazy happening every day. Like, just the other day, I seen yr mark. Not on you. On someone elses arm.   *the monster*

Hester

Whose?

(Rest)
Whose?!?!

Hester
Canary

Canary
—. Cant remember.

Hester
I'll get back at her. Im not a mother otherwise.
(Rest)
I'll get her. And yll help me.

Canary
Lemmie towel you off.

Hester
I'll get her and yll help me. We'll get her together.

Canary
We dont need to do nothing like that. We'll take our bad
luck on the chin.

Hester
Take my bad luck on my chin. No. My chin aint big enough.

Canary
Lets get you dressed.

Hester
Yll help me.

Canary
No. If I help you I'd have to give up the Mayors bed. Theyd
put all the blame on me. Anyway, what can we do? Just us 2?

Hester
I'll get Butcher to help. You and me and him makes 3. 3s the
charm.

Canary
Idunno—

Hester
"Hes dead," they said. "According to our records, hes been
dead for years," they said. "Sorry for the mix-up," they said.
"Yll get a full refund," they said. A full refund aint enough.
(Rest)
Yll help me.

Canary
I'll help you. Whats the plan.

Hester
I dont got one yet.

Canary
Ah.

Hester
I'll think of something. And yll help.

Canary
(Rest)
Sure.

Hester
Good.

> The backdoor bell rings.

Hester
(Rest)
Is tonight all right?

Canary
Tonight?!

Hester
Yes.

Canary
Hester
Canary
Hester

Canary
Tonights fine.

Hester
We'll kidnap her and toss her off a cliff! How does that sound?
(Rest)
Wait here. Be ready. I'll talk to Butcher.

Canary
I remember whose arm it was. That Monster convict
Remember I told you I saw him at the sea lookout?

Hester
Hes an evil person.

Canary
With a scar like yours.

Hester
Which goes to show that mothers all over the world bite
their sons. Boy tried to be good his whole life and now his
mother weeps. I wonder what that evil Monsters mothers
doing right now. Dancing, I bet.

The bell rings again and again and again.

Hester
I wont be gone for long. Be ready.

Hester leaves. Canary sits there.

SCENE 16

The Hunters walk across the stage.

First Hunter
Peoplev seen em.

Third Hunter
That streetwalker gave us a piece of his shirt.

Second Hunter
Plus that anonymous tip: "ocean overlook at midnight."

First Hunter
We'll catch him before morning. The dogs have the scent.

Third Hunter
Cept theyre going around in circles.

Second Hunter
We'll catch him tonight. We'll show him what it means to be a Hunter.

They continue on their way.

SCENE 17

Butchers place. Meat hanging around on meat hooks.
Butcher at his butchers block hacking away
at a piece of meat. Hester sitting there watching.

Butcher
This is violent. I know. It must be upsetting to you after
everything thats happened. Its an order for Hizzoner.

Hester
You delivering it?

Butcher
Hes picking it up himself. Its his day to rub shoulders with
the people.

Hester
I dont want him to rub my shoulder.

Butcher
Stand over there when he comes. He wont notice you.
(Rest)
I was on my way over. I got some flowers for you back in the
meat cooler. You should be in bed—

Hester
I need yr help.

Butcher
Ask away. Wait: here he comes.

As Hester steps into the shadows,
the Mayor enters with his basket.

Butcher
Good to see you, sir.

Mayor
The local butcher at his chopping block. Hard honest
worker. Thats what I like to see.

Butcher
Ive got yr order right here.

Mayor
Im passing out cigars. Have one.

Butcher
Thank you.

Mayor
My First Lady and I are expecting. A child.

Hester
(A child.)

Mayor
You heard right.

Hester
(A child!)

Mayor
Thats right. She begged me to keep it hush-hush but I cant
help myself. I feel that its my duty to share the news.

Butcher
Congratulations.

Hester
(A child!)

Mayor
My wife with child. That makes me a father.

Butcher
Congratulations.

Hester
(A child.)

Mayor
I want to weep.

Hester
((You will.))

Mayor
Whadyasay?

Butcher
Nothing.
(Rest)
Yr meat.

Mayor
Thank you. Until next week.

Butcher
Until next week.

>   Mayor leaves. Hester comes out of hiding.

Butcher
They finally got lucky.

Hester
Hester

Butcher
Hester?

Hester
Sweetheart.

Butcher
I wish them luck.

Hester
So do I.

Butcher
After everything thats happened?

Hester
I wish them luck.

Butcher
Yr an angel.

Hester
I need yr help.

Butcher
Anything my angel wants. But first:
(Rest)
I earn a good living. And I still have my looks. There are a
lot of women who wink at the Meat Man and I know what
theyre thinking. Word is Im a catch.

> He stands at his butcher block and sings
> "A Meat Man Is a Good Man to Marry":

Butcher
A Meat Man is a good man to marry
The wife of a Meat Man dont worry
The children will never go hungry
Always plenty of meat in the tummy.

A Meat Man, his livestock are friendly
They go to the slaughter full knowing
He will kill them and carve them most kindly
In our stomachs theyll help us keep growing.

With me yr mate, everyday we'll have steak
Gizzards, chittlins and chops

Come on, lets tie the knot.
Pork, beef, mutton, yll be my only one
Pig tails and feet and snouts
We'll kiss day in and out.
Make me yr ball and chain
We'll dine on fried brain.

And what could ever beat a honey-dear
Who can make a silk purse from a sow's ear?

The wife of a Meat Man is happy
All her days are so sunny and easy.
All her nights full of hot heavy breathing
And love
Cause a Meat Mans the best man to marry.

Butcher
Hester

> He leaves his butcher block and comes over to her.

Butcher
Marry me.   ✗ i are about marriage

Hester
I need yr help. With the First Lady.
(Rest)
I wanna talk to her is all.

Butcher
And you want me to help you think of what to say.

Hester
Shes shy about being seen with me. Her position, you know
and everything thats happened. She wants to come to my
house but dont want no one to know.
(Rest)
I need you to drive your truck. Tonight. Say some of the
order was forgotten and yr delivering it. Canary will be waiting there with her. The First Lady aint been feeling well as
of late so she may be—foggy, but dont let that stop you.

Dont let nothing stop you. She wants to talk tonight. Shes real insistent. And she dont want no one knowing. Bring her to me, let us talk then take her home again thats all.

Butcher
Whatll you talk about?

Hester
Just chitchat. Woman to woman stuff. I have a feeling she wants to apologize. Maybe even give me some sort of—payment for my hardships. Go get her around 11. Itll be dark. No onell see. Then take her home around midnight.
(Rest)
We need to have a talk, her and me, thats all, just a talk, woman to woman, her and me. Yll help?

Butcher
Sure.
(Rest)
Then we'll get married.

Hester
Then we'll get married.

> He tries to hug her. She gently pulls away.

Hester
Mmnot ready for touching yet. I need to go home.

Butcher
I'll walk you.

Hester
No thanks.
(Rest)
After me and her talk. We can be together then.

> He tries to kiss her cheek. She goes. He goes back to his chopping block but just stands there.

SCENE 18

3 Freshly Freed Prisoners singing "Hard Times":

Freshly Freed Prisoners
I done hard time on this earth
Hard time on the rock pile
Hard time behind the bars
And now at last Im home.

Is there a face that knows my face?
A voice that knows my name?
Hard times in these free streets
If no one welcomes me.

Hard Times Hard Times
Hard Times Hard Times
Hard Times, if ya followed me this far,
I'll just lay down and die.

SCENE 19

Hesters place. Its dark. The room is dimly lit.
She readies her tools.

Hester
Ready yr tools, Hester. Prepare yr instruments. Sharpen yr
knives, clean yr hoses, boil yr water, check the strength of
yr straps. Itll be easy. She wont feel nothing. Not right away.
And she'll wake up tomorrow bloody and wondering whered
the baby go? But no. She wont know.
(Rest)
Rip her child from her like she ripped mine from me.
(Rest)
Shes expecting. But shes not expecting this.

Someone stands in her back doorway.

Hester
Im closed tonight. Yll have to come back tomorrow.

Monster comes in.

Hester
Tell yr wife Im closed.

Monster
Im lost.

Hester
I cant help you tonight.

Monster
I got out of prison just now. You heard us singing.

Hester
I heard. Huh. You look familiar. A little. Im real busy just now—

song?

Monster
I got out of jail alive. Ive got the personal effects of a friend of mine who died in there. I promised him I'd bring them to his mother. They gave me directions but I lost my way.

Hester
Where ya headed?

Monster
"The Rich Girls House." She must be a rich woman now but "The Rich Girls House" was all he said.

Hester
Go back to the square. Someonell point the way.

Monster
My friends mother. She works for them. Scrubbing floors.

Hester
Scrubbing floors.

Monster
Yeah.
(Rest)
He was Smith. Her too.
(Rest)
Why are you staring?

Hester
No reason.

Monster
Yr circling me.

Hester
You look familiar.

Monster
Yr busy. I'll leave you—

Hester
Wait! His effects. Lemmie see. Just a peek. Im curious.

Monster
Theres not much. Just a tin cup. And a spoon. See?

                                   He shows her the cup and spoon.

Hester
(Rest)
Tin cup and spoon, you dont look like Boy Smith at all but
yll have to be enough to remember him by.
(Rest)
Dear son. This is all thats left.
(Rest)
Im his mother. Im his dead mother because hes dead.

Monster
He told me you worked at the Rich—

Hester
The dead Boys dead mother works for herself now. Shes an
aborter. Dont hang yr head shes not yr mom. My fucking A.
He woulda hated what his mother has become. for him.

Monster
No.
(Rest)
I'll tell you stories about him.

Hester
Not now. Its a busy night for me.
(Rest)
My A. My tin cup. My spoon. And you. I know you.

Monster
Yr sons alive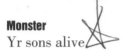

Hester
I heard you described.

Monster
He needs yr help.

Hester
Posters hung all over town.

Monster
Hes as alive as I am.

Hester
Yr Monster! Help! Help!

Monster
Quiet!

Hester
Let go of me! Help!

Monster
Shut up! Shut up!

He subdues her.

Monster
Look. My mark.
(Rest)
You marked me years ago. Its just like yours. Look.

Hester
I marked my *son.* He was good and then he died. Youve got
an ugly scar and yr looking for a hiding place.

Monster
The letters you wrote him—me. Ive got them all.

Hester
Because he gave them to you.

Monster
Because you wrote them to me. I know them all by heart. I'll recite, you read along.

Hester
Cant. Dont need to. Monster. *Evil!* Thats what you are. Ive heard the news. Go on, kill me! Do what ever it is you do! Get it over with!

> He releases her.

Monster
(Rest)
Mother.

> She hurriedly takes up her old shotgun
> and points it at him.

Hester
My son was good. This is a gun. Run.

> She backs him toward the back door and he runs off.
> She puts the gun down and goes
> over to the table to examine the tin cup,
> the spoon and those letters.
> Butchers truck is heard pulling up.

Hester
Trinkets. Maybe from my Boy, maybe not.
(Rest)
My mark looks like a heart. His looked horrid. Like a gash.

> Canary and Butcher at the front door.
> They hold First Lady between them.

Hester
Come in before yr seen.

Butcher and Canary come in
escorting a groggy First Lady.

Butcher
Shes ill.

Hester
Its probably just a dizzy spell.

Canary
Lets sit her in the chair.

They sit her down.

Butcher
Looks worse than a dizzy spell.

Hester
The rich get dizzy all the time. And the richer they are the
dizzier they get.

First Lady
He wanted money but I snitched. Ha.

Butcher
Shes been saying that the whole ride.

First Lady
I snitched I snitched I snitched.

Hester
Come with me, madam. Right this way. Come in here and
we'll have our talk.

Butcher
I'll help you—

Hester
Ive got her. Canary, keep Butcher company.

Canary
Whats this stuff here?

Hester
Just some garbage.

Canary
Theyre letters you wrote to Boy. Says so right here.

Hester
Canary

First Lady
I snitched. I snitched.

Canary
Jamah, Hester, jamah?

Hester
Doht.

Canary
Jamah?

Butcher
No fair you two Talking in front of me. Uh, *noonka Talking-mehnavee.* No fair.

Hester
A friend of his brought them by. *Le traja Scrapeahdepth woah-ya, C-Mary.*

Canary
Scrapeahdepth?

Hester
Di.

First Lady
I snitched. I snitched.

Butcher
Dont mind me, I'll just sit here. Wheres yr radio?

Hester
Stolen.

Canary
Cha Eyeyaya s eh cha Muka vee chet-la Scrapeahdepth ey cocodi Scrapeahdepth. Hester—

Hester
Chet-la eye brack zeemeh. Zeemeh.

Canary
Hester
Canary
Hester

The churchbells announce the hour. 12 midnight.

Hester
Ha! You see what motherlove can do? Get in yr head and make you see all sorts of things.
(Rest)
Come on, maam. Entertain yrselves, we'll be quick.

Hester and First Lady go into the back room, leaving Butcher and Canary.

Canary
She'll open the back door. The fresh airll perk her right up.

Butcher
What were you two talking about?

Canary
This and that.

Butcher
She looked troubled.

Canary
Shes just tired.

Butcher
Whatdoyathink theyre talking about?

Canary
Womens things. Private womens things. Motherhood things.
Things like that. Not for the likes of me to hear. Or you.
(Rest)
Have a drink. I'll rub yr feet.

> He drinks. After removing his socks
> and shoes she rubs his feet.

Butcher
You never had a child?

Canary
Not yet.

Butcher
You oughta get married.

Canary
Naw. Not me.

Butcher
Letters she wrote her son. Poor thing.

Canary
Love her a lot. Love her so much that yr lovell fill up the
wound shes got. Give it a try, K?

Butcher
I plan to.

> First Lady from offstage:

First Lady
Oh!

> Butcher begins to move toward the back room.
> Canary stops him.

Canary

Dont go in there. Sit here with me. Keep me company. You
ever had yr soles read? Lets see: yll live a long life.

Butcher

Will I get married?

Canary

And live happily forever.

Butcher

Whats she doing in there?

Canary

Talking. Let them Talk.
(Rest)
Stay here with me. Please.

Butcher
Canary

First Lady from offstage:

First Lady
Oh!

Canary

Read the letters to me. Go on. We're her friends. Lets pass
the time.

Butcher

"Dear Son, yr 12 today. Thats a lot of years. I thought you
would be out long before now. Every time I go to the Fund
theres another excuse. What can you do? I take it on the
chin and you should too because I know that you get points
for good behavior. Next year yll be 13 and back at home and
we will spend the next 13 years having one big long birth-
day party! Wont that—"

Hester comes out. In her haste she forgot
to put on her apron and so her dress and hands

are stained with blood. She stands there. Horrific.
And trumphant. She tosses her bloody tools
in her wash bucket, lights a candle.

Canary
Taht?

Hester
Taht.

Canary gives Hester a kiss on the cheek. Its goodbye.

Canary
*Hester, weh Seven-leagues swich tue ee meh. Ya weh tahrum
sah Dinkydow, eh?*

Hester
I understand.

Canary
Eee sah Le traja scrapeahdepth. Ki bunda-ley?

Hester
Weh _race_. Pabala weh fihnder. Pabala.

Canary
(Rest)
I guess we can take her home now?

Hester
Please.

Canary goes to load First Lady into the truck.
Butcher puts on his shoes and
stands there ready to go.
Hester gets her basket.

Hester
Butcher
Hester
Butcher

As Butcher turns to follow Canary he passes Hester, and she
takes his hand. Her blood-smeared hand bloodies his hand.
They hold hands for a moment and then he lets her hand go
and, walking out through the back room, very thoroughly
wipes the blood off onto his pants.
Hester stands there with her basket.

Hester
Hester
Hester

After a moment his truck is heard pulling off.
Hester hurries around the room
stuffing things into her basket.

Hester
Hes not. He couldnt be. But what if he is. Monster. He isnt.
But he could be. Although hes not. You know hes not. Just
wanna make sure. See that mark again. Yr motherlove is
playing with yr mind, thats all. Or it is him. Maybe. What
does a monster need. Food. Money. Clothes. More money.
I'll get Butcher to hide him. He wont like the idea at first
cause hes law abiding but lovell take care of that. Maybe.
Butcherll hide him good. Somehow.

We can hear dogs barking in the distance.
Monster is standing in her front doorway.

Monster
Mother.

Hester
Monster

Monster
Mother.

Hester
Monster

Monster
Mother.

216   Suzan-Lori Parks

Hester
Son.

Monster
Theyre on my trail.

Hester
Why would anyone want to catch you?

Monster
Theyve got my scent. She snitched. One of the dogs bit me.
But I had my knife and got him good. They bit me but I cut
them. I ran but their blood and my blood—. Mother?
Mother?

Hester
Yr all grown up. Yr bleeding.

Monster
Theyre bleeding too.

Hester
We'll turn out the lights and theyll think nobodys home and
theyll go away. Theyll go look somewheres else. Theyll go
away. Theyll go away wont they?

Monster
I dont think so.

Hester
Theyll come to the door and I'll tell them I aint seen you.
"What the hell would I be doing seeing a villian like that,"
I'll say. Then theyll go away. Then yll run out the back.

Monster
They wont go away. Theyre hunters. They hunt. They can
smell me. Theyre hunters and they can smell me. They wont
go away. Theyll do what they got to do to catch the Monster.

Hester
Monster

Hester

You used to be so good. What happened?

Monster

Oh—this and that.

(Rest)

Better a monster than a boy. I made something of myself. It wasnt hard.

He sings "The Making of a Monster":

Monster

Youd think itd be hard
To make something horrid
Its easy.

Youd think it would take
So much work to create
The Devil Incarnate
Its easy.

The smallest seed grows to a tree
A grain of sand pearls in an oyster
A small bit of hate in a heart will inflate
And thats more so much more than enough
To make you a Monster.

Youd think itd be hard
To make something horrid
Its easy.

The sound of dogs barking gets louder.

Monster

When they catch me theyll hurt me. Run me through and plant me in yr front yard so you can hear me scream. They catch me and theyll run me through. You hide me theyll run you through too. I wonder how much itll hurt? Theyll keep me alive and cut me up and I wonder how much itll hurt?

(Rest)

Hear the dogs? Take the gun. Shoot me with it.

Hester
Dont be silly.

Monster
Us killing me is better than them killing me.

Hester
You were always so silly.

> The sound of dogs barking gets louder.

Monster
I heard once how they cut one guys balls off and let him watch the dogs eat them and then they cut his fingers off and the dogs ate those and he had to watch. His fingers and then his toes then his feet then his hands.
(Rest)
Please.

Hester
Hester

Monster
Please.

> The sound of the dogs barking is very loud.
> The Hunters voices are heard.
> Hester and Monster sit close together.
> They hold their arms side by side,
> comparing their bite marks.

Hester
Monster
Hester
Monster
Hester
Monster

Hester
I have a way to do it that wont hurt.
(Rest)
Give me yr knife. Sit in my lap.

She sits in a chair. He hands her his knife and sits on the floor
in front of her with his back toward her stomach.
She gently pets his head. Then, with a quick firm motion,
she slits his throat like Butcher taught her.
He dies. She holds him in her lap.
The sound of dogs barking and
Hunters voices are now deafening.
Theyre right outside her door. They force their way in.
They stand around looking at Hester and Monster.
The dogs bay outside.

She aborted her child

First Hunter
Its him!

Second Hunter
But hes dead!

Third Hunter
Too bad!

First Hunter
Plenty of fun still to be had, though!

Third Hunter
Hes still warm.
(Rest)
Hes ours by rights, gal. Give him up.

First Hunter
If you think yll get any of the reward money, you got another
thing coming.

The Hunters leave dragging Monsters body.
Hester sits there alone.
She gets up, drops the knife in the wash bucket.
She lights another candle. She sits down.

Hester
Hester
Hester

Hester sings "Working Womans Song (Reprise)":

Hester
I dig my ditch with no complaining
Work in the hot sun, or even when its raining
And when the bitter day finally comes to an end
Theyll say—

 She sits there unable to continue.

Hester
Hester
Hester

 After a moment, the ~~backdoor bell rings insistently.~~
 She ignores it.
 It rings again, more insistently.
 She gets up and puts on her apron,
 then wearily sits back down.
 After a moment the bell rings again.

Hester
Hester
Hester

 She gets up, picks up her tools and goes back to work.

 End of Play

TALK Translation

Part One, Scene 1, Page 117

die Abah-nazip.	The abortion.

Page 119

Die la-sah Chung-chung? . . . woah-ya.	And her pussy? Her pussy is so disgusting, so slack, so very very completely dried out.
seh tum . . . woah-ya	Yr pussy is all dried out!
teeh tum-ay . . . oromakeum!	You got a respectable good-for-nothing vagina!

Page 124

falltima . . . woah-ya.	When her period comes she is in hysterics

Page 125

die Abah-nazip.	The abortion.

Scene 2, Page 127

Papameh! . . . ma-Ovo!	Pity me! I got my period again!

Page 128

Meh Kazo-say . . . ee—	My vagina is nice and pleasant and—

Scene 3, Page 132

die Abah-nazip.	The abortion.

tee-tee . . . Zoo.	They open their legs for anybody and everybody.
Hee la . . . nice-like.	As if their vaginas were their mouths.
Hi-Chungwoah! . . . Baza.	Their vaginas are like common sewers.
Woah-ya dateh.	I totally agree with you.

Scene 5, Page 146

Le doe-dunk . . . hunter.	You force yrself on yr wife and then you send her to me, Mister Hunter.

Scene 6, Page 149

Suptah nekkie . . . Noonke!	You and yr slack dried-up prissy pussy! No one would be caught dead inside such a stupid twat! May you never conceive! May yr womb dry up and shrivel! May yr tubes tie themselves in knots! May yr egg sacks be forever empty! May yr breasts shrivel and never ever give milk!

Scene 7, Page 151

kaltie Bleehc	Chilly twat

Part Two, Scene 14, Page 189

Weh noonka . . . rum—	I missed my period. I stuck something up there, but—
Weh nim . . . rum—	I took one of them tests. It said "not pregnant," but—
Weh nam . . . woah.	I dont bother with the tests. Theyre so expensive and my man says, they lie anyway.
Tah humble.	Yr showing.
Tah humble si.	Yr showing too.

Scene 19, Page 211

Jamah, Hester, jamah?   Hester, whats the matter?

Doht.   Nothing.

Jamah?   What is it?

noonka . . . mehnavee.   I couldnt speak TALK to save my life.

Le traja . . . . C-Mary   He had a very odd-looking scar.

Scrapeahdepth?   An odd-looking scar?

Di.   Yeah.

Page 212

Cha Eyeyaya . . . Hester.   The look on yr face says the scar wasnt just any scar, Hester—

Chet-la . . . Zeemeh.   It looked like mine, it did. It did.

Page 215

Taht?   Is it done?

Tuht.   Its done.

Hester, weh . . .
Dinkydow, eh?   Im going to have to keep my distance from you for a while. To avoid suspicion, you understand?

Eee sah . . . bunda-ley?   What will you do about the man with the odd looking scar?

Weh <u>race</u>. . . . Pabala.   I'll dash out of here. Maybe I'll find him. Maybe.

Working Womans Song

Hester, Canary

Words and Music by Suzan-Lori Parks

"Here is a wo-man who does all she can."

My Little Army
Mayor

Words and Music by Suzan-Lori Parks

CUE: . . . all those little men swimming.

MAYOR: An army! My own little private army! Loy-al-ty is the most im-

por-tant thing in an ar-my, and my men have loy-al-ty to me. They will

lay down their lives so our state will sur-vive. I find that kind of cour-age ve-ry

char-ming. I sa- lute the men of my lit-tle ar-my.

The Hunters Creed

Hunters

Words and Music by Suzan-Lori Parks

Gilded Cage
Canary

Words and Music by Suzan-Lori Parks

free and brave. But in my dream——— she spoke to me from a

gor- geous gil- ded cage. Her

gil- ded cage was so- lid gold, the bars shone like sun- shine.

She'd gone in there all on her own,— no one had forced her

this time. "Free-dom," she said,— "ain't free at all. Its price: a

heavy wage. And when you find how much your free- dom costs, you

just may give it up for a gor- geous gil- ded cage."

My Vengeance

Hester

Words and Music by Suzan-Lori Parks

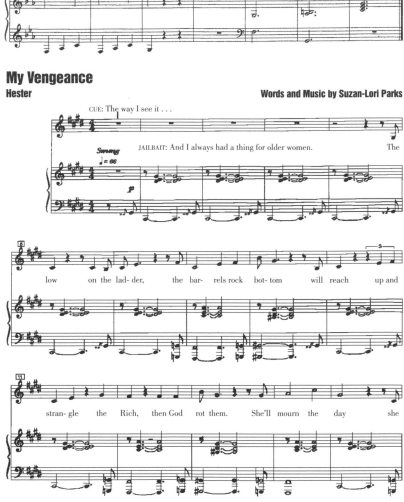

CUE: The way I see it . . .

JAILBAIT: And I always had a thing for older women. The

low on the lad- der, the bar- rels rock bot- tom will reach up and

stran- gle the Rich, then God rot them. She'll mourn the day she

My Little Enemy

First Lady

Words and Music by Suzan-Lori Parks

CUE: Smart thinking.

WW#2: Real real smart thinking. They say Fi- de- li- ty is the most im-

por- tant thing when yr mar- ried. But its such a pri-cey lux-u- ry. When yr

up a-gainst— the wall,—y ll take a poke from some poor slob. The child Im grow-ing will be my sal-

va-tion. Who knows, he may grow up to rule the na-tion. And my hus-band,

blind with hap-pi-ness,— will nev- er guess— the en-e-my in his ar-my.

A Meat Man Is a Good Man to Marry
Butcher

Words and Music by Suzan-Lori Parks

dine on fried— brain, and what could ev-er beat a ho-ney- dear who can make a silk purse from

a sow's ear? The— wife of a Meat Man is hap- py. All her days are so

sun-ny and ea- sy. all her nights full of hot hea- vy brea-thing and

love,——— cause a Meat Mans the best man to mar- ry.

Hard Times
Freshly Freed Prisoners

Words and Music by Suzan-Lori Parks

I done hard time—— on— this

earth, hard time—— on the rock pi- le, hard time—— be- hind the

bars, and now———— at least Im home————

Is there a face———— that knows my face? A

voice——— that knows my name?— Hard Times———— in these free streets. If

no—— one wel-comes me.——————— Hard——

Times, Hard——— Times, Hard Times,——— Hard Times,——— Hard

Times, If—— ya fol-lowed me this far,——— I'll just lay down and die.

The Making of a Monster
Monster

Words and Music by Suzan-Lori Parks

Working Womans Song (Reprise)

Hester

Words and Music by Suzan-Lori Parks

I dig my ditch with no— com- plain-ing

work in the hot sun, or e-ven when its rain-ing. And when the bitt-er day

fi-nally comes to an end, they'll say— (bell)